SUPER BOWL VICTORIES

by Angelo G. Resciniti

Front cover photo by Heinz Kluetmeier/*SPORTS ILLUSTRATED*
Back cover photo by Andy Hayt/*SPORTS ILLUSTRATED*

Published by Willowisp Press, Inc.
401 E. Wilson Bridge Road, Worthington, Ohio 43085

Printed in the United States of America

10 9 8 7 6 5 4 3 2 1

ISBN 0-87406-038-9

To my super grandfolks, Angelo and Rose Resciniti. They took me to the first Super Bowl game. And they gave me love, always. May God bless them both.

and

To M.H., for a super opportunity. Thanks.

Super Bowl Quiz

1. What team has won more Super Bowls than any other team?
2. What teams have played in more Super Bowls than any other teams?
3. What teams have won two Super Bowls in a row?
4. In which Super Bowl were the most points scored?
5. Who are the only two players to be named Most Valuable Player two years in a row?
6. Who is the only losing player to win Most Valuable Player?
7. When did two players win Most Valuable Player? Who were they?
8. Who has thrown the most touchdown passes in a Super Bowl game?

Turn the page for the answers.

Answers to Quiz

1. *Pittsburgh Steelers—4 times, IX, X, XIII, XIV.*
2. *Dallas Cowboys—5 times, V, VI, X, XII, XIII. Miami Dolphins—5 times, VI, VII, VIII, XVII, XIX.*
3. *Green Bay I, II; Miami Dolphins VII, VIII; Pittsburgh Steelers IX, X, XIII, XIV.*
4. *XIII, Total of 66 points scored.*
5. *Bart Starr, Green Bay Packers I, II; Terry Bradshaw, Pittsburgh Steelers XIII, XIV.*
6. *Chuck Howley, Dallas Cowboys, V.*
7. *Super Bowl XII, Harvey Martin, Randy White, Dallas Cowboys.*
8. *Terry Bradshaw, Pittsburgh Steelers, XIII.*

CONTENTS

SUPER BOWL XIX

The year 1984 was a record-breaking kind of season in the National Football League.

Eric Dickerson, brilliant young runner for the Los Angeles Rams, broke O.J. Simpson's "unbreakable" single-season rushing record.

And Chicago Bears' veteran runner Walter Payton broke Jim Brown's "unbreakable" career rushing record.

In any normal NFL season, Dickerson and Payton would have been the talk of the league. "Unbreakable" records are, after all, remarkable when broken. But 1984 was no normal NFL season. It was the year of "Dangerous Dan" Marino of the Miami Dolphins.

Dickerson and Payton achieved the remarkable. Marino achieved the incredible. The second-year quarterback shattered two of the NFL's oldest records. He became the first NFL quarterback ever to throw more than 5,000 yards in a season. And he tossed a record-exploding 48 touchdown passes. In an *average* game, Marino threw for 320 yards and three touchdowns. That's a career high for many quarterbacks! For Marino, that was just another Sunday at the ball park.

"Dangerous Dan" led his Dolphins to a 14-2 regular season record. The Dolphins ran away with the AFC East title. They scored the most points in the NFL. The Marino-led Dolphins cruised through the playoffs. They ripped Seattle, 31-10, behind four Marino TD passes. They crushed Pittsburgh, 45-28, behind Marino's three scoring tosses. As the Dolphins prepared for Super Bowl XIX, the eyes of the football world were on Dan Marino.

This attention on Marino took attention away from the San Francisco 49ers. The 49ers and their spectacular quarterback, Joe Montana, enjoyed a record-breaking season of their own. Their 15-1 record was the best in the NFL in 1984. And their only loss was by three points. The 49ers handily won the NFC West title. Their defense was the toughest in the NFL. San Francisco opened the playoffs with a 21-10 romp over the New York Giants. Then the 49ers crushed Chicago, 23-0, in the NFC title game.

San Francisco approached Super Bowl XIX with a 17-1 record. A win in the Super Bowl would be the 49ers' eighteenth victory of the season. No NFL team had ever before won more than 17 games in a season. The 49ers were seeking a place in NFL history. But all the fans wanted to talk about was "Dangerous Dan" Marino and the Miami Dolphins.

"All we heard about was the Miami offense

and how were we going to stop it," admitted Joe Montana. "Deep inside, the feeling was, 'We have an offense, too. How is anyone going to stop us?'"

Added Montana, "Yes, we had something to prove."

The odds-makers agreed. They favored the 49ers by three points in the big game.

A crowd of 84,059 filled Stanford Stadium near Palo Alto, California, for Super Bowl XIX. Millions of people world-wide tuned in on television. President Ronald Reagan conducted the coin toss from the White House in Washington, D.C. The weather in California was perfect. The stage was set for a special game.

"Dangerous Dan" Marino and the Dolphins got off to a big start in Super Bowl XIX. Marino's hot hand moved the Dolphins on two scoring drives in the first quarter.

The Dolphins' first possession began on their own 36-yard line. Marino stepped back to pass on the first play. He fired out to running back Tony Nathan in the flat. Nathan juked, spun, and raced downfield for a 25-yard gain. If one play was to mean anything, Marino and the Dolphins were up for a big day. The drive ended in a 37-yard field goal by Uwe von Schamann. Miami took a 3-0 lead.

San Francisco quickly struck back. Montana keyed the 49ers' first TD drive by running and passing. On third-and-seven from Miami's 48, Montana dropped back to pass. Miami defensive end Kim Bokamper barrelled in for the sack. Montana slipped Bokamper's tackle and started running. He raced 15 yards down the sideline for a big first down. On the next play, Montana rolled to the right. Running back Carl Monroe slipped out of the backfield. Montana hit Monroe with a perfect pass. The speedy running back eluded safety Lyle Blackwood's tackle and raced into the end zone. The 33-yard TD and Ray Wersching's extra point gave San Francisco a 7-3 lead.

The Dolphins launched a special plan in their next possession. Miami coach Don Shula knew the 49ers' defense liked to make a lot of substitutions after every play. So Shula ordered Marino to work without a huddle. After every play the Dolphins raced to the line of scrimmage for another snap. This gave San Francisco no time for changes.

The plan worked. Marino hit tight end Dan Johnson with a 21-yard pass. He fired to wide receiver Mark Clayton for 13 yards. He hit wide receiver Mark "Super" Duper with an 11-yard completion. The drive ended with a two-yard touchdown pass from Marino to Johnson. Von Schamann's extra point gave Miami a 10-7 lead.

The first quarter ended at 10-7. The 17 points set a Super Bowl record for the first quarter. Marino completed nine of 10 passes in the period. As expected, Super Bowl XIX was a high-scoring game to this point. And "Dangerous Dan" Marino was having a field day.

Wide World Photos, Inc.

San Francisco 49ers' Roger Craig flies across the goal line for a touchdown against Miami.

But Marino went a little flat on Miami's next possession. And Miami punter Reggie Roby, the best in the NFL, also went flat. His short 37-yard punt set up the 49ers at Miami's 47.

Joe Montana's scrambling hurt Miami once again. The fleet-footed quarterback scrambled for 19 yards on the first play after the bad punt. Montana then passed to wide receiver Dwight Clark for a 16-yard gain. From the Dolphins' eight-yard line Montana hit running back Roger Craig with the touchdown pass. Ray Wersching's kick gave the 49ers a 14-10 lead early in the second quarter.

Another short Reggie Roby punt gave San Francisco the ball at their own 45. It took Montana only six plays to produce another TD. Two of the plays were passes to veteran tight end Russ Francis. Montana scored the touchdown on a scramble from six yards out. Wersching kicked the extra point to give the 49ers a sudden 21-10 lead. Nearly half the second period remained.

Marino continued to have his problems against San Francisco's highly-rated defense. The no-huddle offense no longer worked. The 49ers had adjusted by using an unusual 4-1-6 defense. Four linemen rushed Marino. One linebacker played short pass defense or blitzed the quarterback. Six defensive backs covered Miami's speedy receivers. The defense dared Marino to throw. He kept throwing. He kept coming up empty. And when the Dolphins tried running, San Francisco's defensive line blasted the ball carriers after short gains.

Another short Reggie Roby punt set up another San Francisco touchdown. This drive started at the 49ers's 48-yard line. Nine plays and 52 yards later, Roger Craig blasted over from the three-yard line. Wersching's kick gave San Francisco a huge 28-10 lead. Key plays in the TD drive included a 20-yard pass from Montana to Craig and a nine-yard gain by speedy running back Wendell Tyler.

The Dolphins managed to move the ball on their next possession. Marino hit some short passes and a 30-yard bomb to tight end Joe Rose. The drive ended in a 31-yard von Schamann field goal with 12 seconds left in the first half. The kick cut San Francisco's lead to 28-13.

On the ensuing kickoff, von Schamann bounced a short, careening kick at the 49ers. Guard Guy McIntyre smothered the ball. The half should have ended there. But McIntyre rose up and started to run. He was smashed by Miami's Joe Carter. The football popped loose. Miami's Jim Jensen recovered the shocking fumble. Von Schamann kicked a 30-yard field goal with four seconds left in the half.

The first half ended with San Francisco ahead, 28-16. The 49ers's 28 points and the combined 44 points were new Super Bowl records for scoring in a half.

The Dolphins tried valiantly to come back in the second half. But the San Francisco defense began to dominate the game. The 4-1-6 defense completely shut down Miami's running attack. Marino was forced to pass on play after play. Miami's offensive line was forced into strength-draining pass blocking on play after play. Soon the weary linemen started giving ground to San Francisco's brutal pass rush. Marino found himself surrounded by red-and-gold uniforms on every pass play. He rushed his passes. He tried to scramble. He threw too long. He threw too short.

The sacks began in the second half. Dwaine Board got to Marino twice. Manu Tuiasosopo and Gary "Big Hands" Johnson each sacked Marino once. Four sacks against Miami was big news. The Dolphins allowed only 14 sacks in 18 games prior to Super Bowl XIX.

And with the sacks came the interceptions. Eric Wright made an acrobatic interception to save a touchdown pass in the third quarter. Carlton Williamson stole a misguided Marino aerial in the end zone in the fourth quarter. For the first time in his pro career, Marino threw more interceptions (2) than TD passes (1) in a game.

The 49ers scored a field goal in the third quarter to end a 10-play, 43-yard drive. A Montana 12-yard scramble was the key play in the drive. Wersching kicked the 27-yarder to give San Francisco a 31-16 lead.

Montana put together a final drive late in the third quarter. San Francisco started at their own 30-yard line. Montana passed 30 yards to Wendell Tyler and 13 yards to Russ Francis. The drive ended with Montana's third TD pass of the game, 16 yards to Roger Craig. Wersching's kick gave the 49ers a 38-16 lead.

Super Bowl XIX finished as a blow-out. The margin of victory was the second widest in Super Bowl history. The 49ers' 38 points tied the Super Bowl record. While it ended at 38-16, the 49ers could easily have scored more points. They were deep in Miami territory late in the game.

Joe Montana, for the second time in his career, was named Most Valuable Player in the Super Bowl. He completed 24 of 35 passes for a Super Bowl record of 331 yards, and three touchdowns. Additionally, he ran five times for 59 important yards and a touchdown.

Montana became only the third player to win two Super Bowl MVP awards. Bart Starr (Green Bay) and Terry Bradshaw (Pittsburgh) had previously won the double honor.

"That's great company to be in," said a jubilant Montana in the wild 49ers' locker room after the victory.

San Francisco's offensive and defensive units shared the credit for the lopsided victory. The offense ran off 326 net passing yards, 211 rushing yards, and a Super Bowl record 537 total yards. The defense allowed the fewest rushing yards in Super Bowl history (25) and forced superstar quarterback Dan Marino into his worst outing of the season.

The 49ers' coach, Bill Walsh, clutched the

Vince Lombardi Trophy afterward and praised his team. He called the 49ers' team "the greatest [team] playing football today. And our defense is one of the best, if not *the* best, in football. We were superior defensively and it showed."

"We're the best," crowed team owner Eddie DeBartolo, Jr. "The best. I am proud of putting it together. I am proud of Bill Walsh. This trophy, the Vince Lombardi Trophy, belongs to him, to his assistants, and all these wonderful players."

The players on both teams credited Montana's scrambling and the powerful 49er defense with making the difference.

Montana's 59 yards set a Super Bowl rushing record for quarterbacks.

"He doesn't ever plan to run," said 49ers' assistant coach Paul Hackett. "But it's an option... and a guy with Joe's athletic ability can make it a good option."

"None of it's by design," added Montana. "Most of the time it's just something that happens. A play breaks down, a big hole just opens in front of me, and I just take off."

"Joe Montana had his greatest game of the year," said Bill Walsh. "And the fact that we put the pressure on Marino made a lot of difference."

"We thought that if we could put enough pressure up front, we could rattle Marino," said defensive end Fred Dean.

"It's hard to throw when you have [our] guys banging on you all the time," said cornerback Ronnie Lott. "It's easy to lose your composure."

"Dangerous Dan" Marino may have lost his composure and the ball game, but he set two Super Bowl records. His 50 passes and 29 completions were both records. But Marino and the rest of the quiet, down-hearted Dolphins wanted victory, not records.

"They did what they had to do to stop us," said Marino. "They took us out of our scheme. They came after us with a four-man rush. And it's very difficult to throw against six or seven defensive backs.

"It's going to be tough to live with," added the 23-year-old Marino. "But we'll look at the good things and at the same time tip our hats to the 49ers. They were outstanding. It really hurts that we can't be the world champions. When you get this far, you want to do well. You want to win. Hopefully we'll be back and have another opportunity."

"When you get beat the way we got beat, you take your hat off to the victor, and that's what I'm going to do," said Miami head coach Don Shula. "The disappointment of not getting it done will be with all of us. But you don't get discouraged about something like this. You have to think about the accomplishments we had this year."

The Dolphins accomplished a fine 16-3 record for the long season. San Francisco ended up with the record-setting 18-1 mark. Between them the teams set 25 new Super Bowl records and tied eight more in Super Bowl XIX.

Even as the locker rooms emptied and the

parties began, talk returned to the quarterbacks, to "Dangerous Dan" Marino and MVP Joe Montana.

"He's still a great quarterback," said Montana of Marino.

"Marino will have his day," said Bill Walsh after his second Super Bowl victory as 49ers' coach. "But Joe Montana is the best quarterback in the game today and maybe of all time."

On that special Sunday, anyway, no one would have dared disagree with the winning coach in Super Bowl XIX.

	1stQ	2ndQ	3rdQ	4thQ		Final
Miami	10	6	0	0	—	16
San Francisco	7	21	10	0	—	38

Miami — FG von Schamann 37
SF — Monroe 33 pass from Montana (Wersching kick)
Miami — Johnson 2 pass from Marino (von Schamann kick)
SF — Craig 8 pass from Montana (Wersching kick)
SF — Montana 6 run (Wersching kick)
SF — Craig 3 run (Wersching kick)
Miami — FG von Schamann 31
Miami — FG von Schamann 30
SF — FG Wersching 27
SF — Craig 16 pass from Montana (Wersching kick)
Attendance — 84,059

SUPER BOWL XVIII

Somewhere down the line, Marcus Allen got a bum rap. Somebody somewhere, somehow, decided that the award-winning running back wouldn't cut it in the National Football League. They said he wasn't fast enough, that he'd never break the long gainers. They said he'd never be a game-breaker.

The bum rap started during Allen's senior year at the University of Southern California. USC had long been the home of great running backs, from O.J. Simpson to Greg Pruitt to Charles White. All of them were Heisman Trophy winners. Allen rushed for an incredible 2,342 yards in 1981, his senior season. He earned the Heisman Trophy. He was generally considered the best player in college football.

When the 1982 NFL draft came around, team after team passed over Marcus Allen. The word was out. The 6-foot-1, 210-pound Allen was too slow to star in the NFL.

"A lot of people said I couldn't go the distance," remembered Allen. "They said I wasn't fast enough."

Sixteen teams passed over Allen in the 1982

draft. Finally, the Los Angeles Raiders drafted the Heisman Trophy winner as the seventeenth pick in the first round. Allen was a typical Raider selection. The Raiders' "bad boy" image was built around guys who were either too small, too slow, too weird, or too old to cut it with other teams. Nothing gets a player up for a game better than the opportunity to show the football world that it was wrong, that the player can still hit with the best of them.

"The rap on Marcus is speed," said Pruitt, by this time an aging veteran. Some folks had said Pruitt was washed up. So, naturally, he became a Raider and led the league in returning punts. "I wanted him to prove people wrong just as I had."

Allen provided some proof during the strike-shortened 1982 season. He rushed for 697 yards. He earned Rookie of the Year honors. He became the only rookie to start in the Pro Bowl.

In 1983, Allen ran for 1,014 yards and nine touchdowns. He helped the Raiders to a 12-4 regular season record. The Raiders won the AFC West title. Marcus really turned it on in the playoffs. He gained 121 yards in a 38-10 slaughter of the Pittsburgh Steelers. Then, in the AFC title game, he busted for 154 yards against the Seattle Seahawks. Los Angeles won the game, 30-14, avenging two regular season losses to the Seahawks.

The Raiders headed for Super Bowl XVIII, and Allen was ready. Only problem was that the

Washington Redskins were ready, too. The Redskins were the defending Super Bowl champions. Washington had roared through a 14-2 regular season, with both losses by a single point. The Redskins crushed the Los Angeles Rams by 51-7 to open the playoffs. Then they edged an excellent San Francisco 49ers team, 24-21, in the NFC title game.

The Redskins brought a quest for the record book with them to Super Bowl XVIII. Only two teams had ever won back-to-back Super Bowls, the Pittsburgh Steelers (twice) and the Miami Dolphins. The Redskins, winners of Super Bowl XVII, wanted to be the third team to win back-to-back Super Bowls. The Redskins also wanted to become the first team since 1972 (and the second team ever) to win 17 games in a single NFL season.

Not only were the Raiders fighting history, but also they were fighting the statistics. The Redskins were the very best team in the league in rushing defense. Washington allowed only 81 yards per game. If Marcus Allen was to prove himself to the football world, it would be against the finest defense the NFL had to offer.

A crowd of 72,920 jammed into Tampa Stadium for that Florida city's first-ever Super Bowl. The weather was warm. A brisk breeze gusted up to 20 miles per hour. Passing would be iffy at times. The wind put even more pressure on the running game. At kickoff, the Redskins were favored by three points.

The first break in Super Bowl XVIII went to the Raiders. The Redskins failed to move the ball on their first possession. Jeff Hayes set up to punt on fourth down from the Redskins' 30-yard line. The snap from center Jeff Bostic was high, but Hayes pulled it down. As a result, Hayes was a half-step slow in getting off the punt. By then, Raiders' special teams captain Derrick Jensen had smashed up the middle. Jensen blocked the punt. The ball caromed toward the goal line. There was a huge pileup in the end zone. At the bottom of the pile, cradling the football, was Derrick Jensen. Touchdown, Raiders! Chris Bahr's kick gave Los Angeles a 7-0 lead only five minutes into the game.

The Redskins picked up a fumble of their own on the next punt play. But the drive stalled, and Mark Moseley missed a 44-yard field goal attempt.

The Raiders had the wind to their backs in the second quarter. Quarterback Jim Plunkett started airing out the football. Plunkett lobbed a bomb to wide receiver Cliff Branch for a 50-yard gain. That put the ball on Washington's 15-yard line. Two plays later Plunkett found Branch alone in the end zone. The 13-yard TD pass and Bahr's kick gave Los Angeles a 14-0 lead. Less than six minutes remained in the first half.

Washington responded with its first long drive of the half. Quarterback Joe Theismann, throwing against the wind, hit 3-of-5 passes in marching the 'Skins down the field. The key play was an 18-yard completion to Alvin Garrett. The drive stalled at the Los Angeles seven-yard line. Moseley chipped a 24-yard field goal. With three minutes left in the first half, the Raiders led the game, 14-3.

The Redskins got the ball back at their own 12-yard line with 12 seconds left in the half. Most teams would have run out the clock at that point. An 11-point deficit at halftime was no big deal in the NFL.

But the Redskins set up for a pass play. Three wide receivers lined up on one side. Theismann dropped back to pass. It looked like a long bomb was in the works. Theismann looked deep. Then he whirled and looked to the left flat. A screen play was forming for running back Joe Washington. Theismann lobbed the pass over the outstretched hands of defensive end Lyle Alzado. The ball fluttered a little. Washington awaited the pass.

Incredibly, a black jersey streaked past Washington. Linebacker Jack Squirek intercepted the soft pass and ran into the end zone. Touchdown, Raiders! Squirek was mobbed by his teammates. Chris Bahr kicked the extra point. The Raiders, shockingly, had a 21-3 lead with seven seconds left in the half.

The Redskins, stunned by the turn of events, headed for the locker room at halftime. They needed a big comeback. What they didn't need was Marcus Allen becoming a hero. But that's what they got before the second half was over.

The third quarter started favorably for the

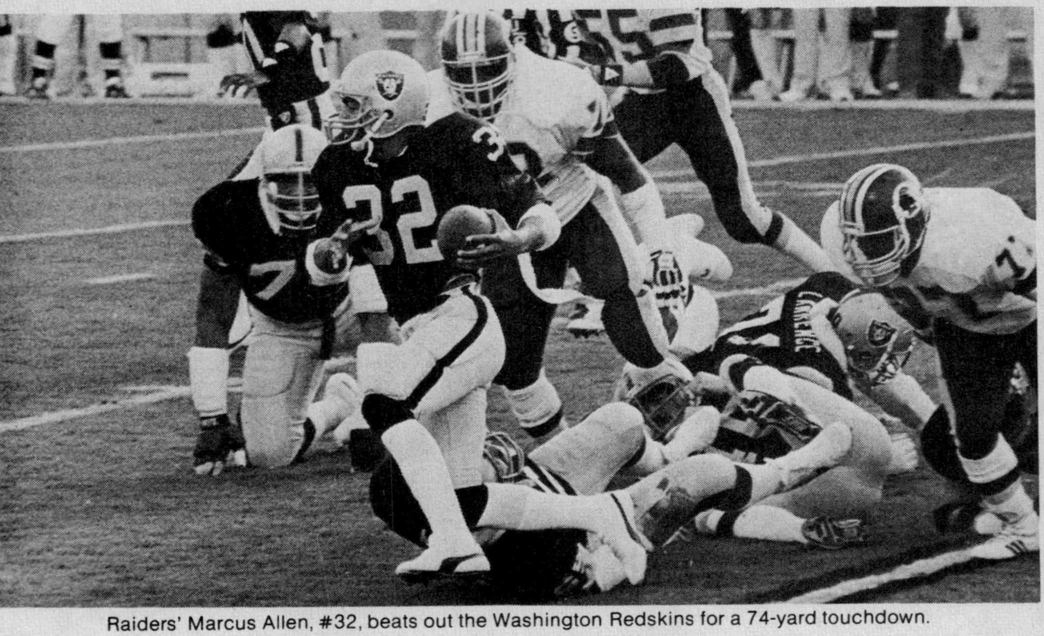

Wide World Photos, Inc.

Raiders' Marcus Allen, #32, beats out the Washington Redskins for a 74-yard touchdown.

Redskins. Theismann marched the 'Skins on a smart 70-yard TD drive. Bullish fullback John Riggins scored the touchdown on a one-yard run. The TD put Riggins in the record books. He became the first player in NFL history to score a touchdown in six straight playoff games. Mark Moseley's extra point try was blocked by tight end Don Hasselback. The Redskins trailed, 21-9, with nearly 11 minutes left in the third quarter. They were still in the game.

The Raiders rose to Washington's challenge. Plunkett led an eight-play, 70-yard drive that ended in a Marcus Allen touchdown run of five yards. Bahr's kick gave Los Angeles a 28-9 lead halfway through the third quarter.

Late in the quarter, Washington recovered a fumble at the Los Angeles 35-yard line. A touchdown would put the Redskins back into the game. After three plays the ball rested on the 26-yard line. It was fourth-and-one. Washington coach, Joe Gibbs, kept the offense on the field. It was make-it-or-break-it time. Theismann handed off to John Riggins. A swarm of black jerseys crashed into Riggins. The Raiders stopped Riggins short of the first down. The ball went over to the Los Angeles offense. There was time for one more play in the third quarter.

And what a play it turned out to be! Plunkett took the snap and handed off to Allen. Led by a pulling guard, Allen started a sweep to the left side. Redskin defenders moved into position for the tackle. So Allen whirled around and started back to the right. He slipped a tackle behind the line of scrimmage. A wall of black-jerseyed blockers set up in front of him. Suddenly he was in the clear. Allen galloped untouched for a 74-yard touchdown. The man called "too slow" had just made the longest TD run in the history of the Super Bowl and in the history of NFL playoffs.

"The first thing I said to him when I caught up with him in the end zone was 'You're not supposed to be this fast. What are you doing in the end zone?'" laughed Greg Pruitt afterward.

Chris Bahr's kick ended the third quarter. The Raiders led, 35-9.

Allen provided all of the excitement in an otherwise-dull fourth quarter. He broke off a 39-yard gain late in the game to set up a Bahr field goal. The three-pointer gave the Raiders a 38-9 lead.

And that's how the game ended. The 38 points were the most ever scored in a Super Bowl game. The 29-point margin of victory was the widest in Super Bowl history. A total of 11 Super Bowl records were set.

The major records belonged to Marcus Allen. He carried the ball 20 times for a Super Bowl record 191 yards and scored two touchdowns. To the surprise of no one, Marcus Allen was named Most Valuable Player of Super Bowl XVIII.

"The MVP?" smiled Allen in the uproarious Raiders' locker room after the game. "I thought about it, but I just wanted the win. The award was just icing on the cake."

"Marcus Allen is a great back," praised Redskins linebacker Neil Olkewicz. "It wasn't so much that we didn't do our jobs. He just made great cuts and great runs."

"He's like watching a gazelle on the plains of Africa," said Raiders lineman Bruce Davis, who blocked all afternoon for Allen.

Marcus Allen's bum rap days were over for good.

Quarterback Jim Plunkett, MVP in Super Bowl XV, had another fine outing in the rout of the Redskins. Plunkett completed 16 of 25 passes for 172 yards and one touchdown. As in Super Bowl XV, Plunkett threw no interceptions. That put him in the Super Bowl record book.

"We were totally prepared and took it to them from the start," celebrated Plunkett. "Everything about the game we dominated. I never expected to handle them the way we did. But one thing I've learned is to never underestimate the Raiders."

Plunkett's main target was wide receiver Cliff Branch. Branch caught six passes for 94 yards and one touchdown. The TD was Branch's third in Super Bowl play, tying him for the career lead. He earlier took the career lead in Super Bowl receptions.

Most of the Raiders and Redskins agreed that the key plays were Jensen's blocked punt, Squirek's interception, and Allen's breakaway run.

"I had a great angle," said Jensen of his block

and touchdown. "The play obviously did not win the game. But it got us off to a good start."

"By the time I had the ball in my hand, he [Jensen] could've grabbed it off my foot," lamented 'Skins punter Jeff Hayes. "We never touched him. They had it set up perfectly. Give them credit."

"It was a shocking thing," admitted center Jeff Bostic, whose high snap led to the block. It was the first of many holes we dug for ourselves. And when you look at the whole thing, it was one of the smaller holes. Give the Raiders credit. They're the champs."

Squirek delighted in the attention he received after the game. That one interception made him an instant star.

"I was in shock," admitted the young linebacker. "The ball floated right to me. I felt like I was in a dream. I couldn't believe it. When everybody started jumping on me in the end zone, I knew it was real. But I don't think it's hit me yet."

"I never saw their linebacker," said Theismann of Squirek's big play. "I was trying to throw the ball over Alzado's head. I threw it too high and too soft."

"That touchdown just before the half really was demoralizing," added Redskins' defensive back Mark Murphy.

"The blocked punt in the first quarter and the interception for a touchdown just before the half were critical plays," said Redskins' head coach

Joe Gibbs. "But they weren't the only ones."

Many of the critical plays were flubs by the usually high-flying Washington offense. Joe Theismann completed only 16 of 35 passes for 243 yards, no touchdowns, and two interceptions. He was sacked six times. Running star John Riggins was held to 64 yards in 26 carries. This was Riggins' first ever playoff game in which he didn't gain at least 100 rushing yards. Known as the "Smurfs," wide receivers Alvin Garrett, Art Monk, and Charlie Brown caught only five passes among them. The Redskins were held to 283 total yards by the Raiders' tough defense.

"They did a good job on defense, a good job on special teams, a good job on offense, and they deserve to be champions," said Gibbs of the victors. "It was a great game on their part. I don't feel that we played our game and I feel that they were very powerful.

"It's a bitter disappointment for us, but I am still very proud of our team," added the Washington head honcho. "We went 16-3 and won the NFC championship. I just wish we could have won [the Super Bowl]."

Raiders' owner Al Davis and head coach Tom Flores accepted the Vince Lombardi Trophy from NFL Commissioner Pete Rozelle. The Raiders now owned three Super Bowl trophies. Only the Pittsburgh Steelers owned more (four).

"It's magnificent," said Davis. Then he praised Flores, a young coach with two Super Bowl victories in five seasons. "Tom has earned the right to be called one of the great coaches of all time. And this Raiders team is one of the best in the history of football."

"It's very satisfying to dominate a game like we did today," said Flores. "This is probably the most impressive performance any of my teams have had. We beat the defending champions, the best."

All around the locker room, victorious Raiders screamed, yelled, hugged, and exchanged high-five hand slaps. And there were some tears, too.

"This is the first time I've been a champion," said veteran defensive end Lyle Alzado. "And it may be my last. I don't care about the money and the Super Bowl ring, but it's great to be a champion."

"This is the greatest feeling in the world," hooted linebacker Ted Hendricks, who retired after the game.

"There are three things you can count on . . ." finished linebacker Rod Martin, " . . . dying, paying taxes, and the Raiders winning the Super Bowl!"

	1stQ	2ndQ	3rdQ	4thQ		Final
Wash	0	3	6	0	—	9
LA	7	14	14	3	—	38

LA — Jensen recovered blocked punt in end zone (Bahr kick)

LA	—	Branch 12 pass from Plunkett (Bahr kick)
Wash	—	FG Moseley 24
LA	—	Squirek 5 interception return (Bahr kick)
Wash	—	Riggins 1 run (kick blocked)
LA	—	Allen 5 run (Bahr kick)
LA	—	Allen 74 run (Bahr kick)
LA	—	FG Bahr 21

Attendance — 72,290

SUPER BOWL XVII

John Riggins has always traveled to the beat of a different drummer.

There was the time he let his bushy hair grow so long that his helmet couldn't fit over his head.

And there was the time he shaved his head, except for a Mohawk streak running down the middle.

Then there was the time he retired because he was bored with football.

And there was the time he fell sound asleep at a party. But this wasn't just any old party. The Vice President of the United States was there. And Riggins was seated at a table with a Supreme Court Justice. Riggins, clad in a tuxedo, snored loudly during the Vice President's speech.

Finally, there was a whole season in which Riggins declined to be interviewed by journalists. That was during the strike-shortened 1982 season, the season that ended in Super Bowl XVII.

"It's an off-beat tune," said Joe Washington, Riggins' running mate with the Washington Redskins. "Not just boom-boom-de-boom-de-boom-boom-boom. It's more of a boom here and a de-de-boom-boom-boom there. It may sound off-beat to other people. But to Big John, it sounds just right."

And when Riggins was just right, he was the best fullback in the NFL. The 6-foot-2, 235-pound Riggins began his career with the New York Jets. He had a couple of fine seasons with New York. But the big guy came alive after a trade to Washington. His 1,014 yards were fifth highest in the NFC in 1978. His 1,153 yards were sixth highest in the NFC in 1979. He also finished third in the NFC in touchdowns that year. Riggins retired in 1980. The Redskins slumped from 10-6 in 1979 to 6-10 in 1980. Big John returned in top form in 1981. He gained 714 rushing yards and scored 13 touchdowns. The Redskins rebounded to 8-8.

Riggins became a quiet, determined player in 1982. He declined to talk to the media. He concentrated on football. He rushed for 553 yards in the nine games of the strike-shortened season. His bullish running took the pressure off Joe Theismann and the 'Skins' passing attack. Joe Theismann loosened up and led the NFC in passing. The defense rallied behind the reborn offensive attack. Washington allowed the fewest points in the NFL (128) and finished with the league's best record (8-1).

Big John came alive in the playoffs. He reeled off three straight 100-yard rushing games, an NFL record. He helped the Redskins run off victories over Detroit (31-7), Minnesota (21-7), and Dallas (31-17). Riggins' 444 yards in three playoff games helped the Redskins to an 11-1 record and a berth in Super Bowl XVII.

The Miami Dolphins rode a solid defense and big-play offense into a 7-2 regular season in 1982. Young quarterback David Woodley was starting for the first time. Second-year running back Andra Franklin provided most of the ground game. The "Killer Bees" defense dominated the AFC all season long. The Dolphins led the league in pass defense and finished second to the Redskins in scoring defense. The "Killer Bees" paced Miami's playoff victories. The Dolphins shut down quarterback Steve Grogan and the New England Patriots, 28-13. Then Miami's defense crushed Dan Fouts and the San Diego Chargers, 34-13. In the AFC title game, the Dolphins white-washed Richard Todd and the New York Jets, 14-0.

The Dolphins were favored by three points in Super Bowl XVII. This Super Bowl was the second rematch in the history of the big game. Miami beat Washington in Super Bowl VII, 14-7.

A crowd of 103,667 filled California's Rose Bowl for this Super Bowl match-up. The excitement started quickly on this sunny Sunday, with Miami making most of the early noise.

The first touchdown of the game came with stunning quickness. After a slow start and an exchange of punts, Miami had the ball on its own 24-yard line. It was second-and-six. Woodley took the snap and rolled to his right. Woodley pumped once. Then he fired a soft pass into the flat. Wide receiver Jimmy Cefalo caught the ball in the space between cornerback Jeris White and safety Tony Peters. Cefalo faked White and headed down the sideline. Peters missed the tackle. Cefalo, suddenly all alone, cut back into the center of the field and raced for the end zone. None of the Redskins came close to catching the fleet-footed receiver. The 76-yard TD pass play was the second longest in Super Bowl history. Uwe von Schamann's kick gave Miami a shocking 7-0 lead with seven minutes gone in the first quarter.

A Woodley fumble late in the quarter led to Washington's first score. Woodley coughed up the football after a hard hit by defensive end Dexter Manley. Nose tackle Dave Butz recovered the ball at Miami's 46-yard line. From there the Redskins went into a conservative rushing offense. Theismann handed off to Big John Riggins again and again. Riggins bulled for four and five yards a carry. The drive stalled at Miami's 14-yard line. Riggins carried on five of the eight plays in the drive. Mark Moseley kicked a 31-yard field goal to cut Miami's lead to 7-3.

Fulton Walker of Miami juked and jived for an exciting 42-yard return of the ensuing kickoff. The return inspired a Miami drive. Woodley ran the offense through a time-consuming 13-play, 50-yard drive. Miami lost steam at Washington's three-yard line. Miami coach, Don Shula, elected

Wide World Photos, Inc.

Washington's John Riggins, #44, escapes tackle from Miami's Don McNeal, #28. Riggins was named the game's Most Valuable Player.

to go for the field goal. Uwe von Schamann kicked the 20-yarder to give Miami a 10-3 lead. Six minutes remained in the first half.

The Redskins put together their best drive of the half on their next possession. Washington started at its own 20-yard line. Theismann, at the order of coach Joe Gibbs, stuck with the ground game. Seven of the next 10 plays were runs, mostly by Riggins. The runs opened up the passing attack. Theismann hit tight end Rick Walker for 27 yards. Then he hooked up on a screen pass with Riggins for 15 yards. A 12-yard scramble by Theismann moved the ball to Miami's 13. On the first play after the two-minute warning, Theismann hit wide receiver Alvin Garrett with a four-yard touchdown pass. The 11-play, 80-yard drive and Moseley's kick tied up the game at 10-10.

The tie didn't last very long. Fulton Walker accepted Moseley's kickoff at the two-yard line. He started to the right. Then he cut back to the left. Steve Shull mowed down one Redskin. Walker put the move on the kicker. The speedy Dolphin suddenly broke into the open. He raced 98 yards for a touchdown, the longest kickoff return in Super Bowl history.

"My first reaction when it was over was to look for a flag," admitted Walker afterward. There were no flags. The exciting touchdown play stood up. Von Schamann kicked the extra point. Miami led 17-10 with 1:38 left in the half.

The Redskins did not simply run out the clock

after that. Theismann led the Washington offense in a perfect, quickly-paced drive down the field. Perfect, that is, until the very end. With 14 seconds left in the half, and no time-outs remaining, Theismann hit Alvin Garrett with a pass at Miami's seven-yard line. Garrett struggled to get out of bounds in order to stop the clock. The Dolphins tackled him on the field. The clock ticked down. Washington's field goal team was still setting up when the half ended. The Redskins lost out on a sure field goal. The half ended with Miami ahead, 17-10.

"I knew I made a stupid play," admitted Joe Theismann later.

"I told them at the half that we have been in tighter situations than this, and won," said Gibbs after the game. "I told them that if we are worth being champions, we will play like champions in the second half."

Washington's defense, strong in the first half, became unbeatable in the third quarter. The 'Skins, in fact, so completely shut down Woodley that he didn't complete another pass in the entire game. And while the defense was dominant, Washington's offense slowly built a momentum of its own.

A trick play led to the only score of the third quarter. Theismann took the snap at his own 47-yard line. He faked the handoff. Then he pitched back to wide receiver Alvin Garrett on the reverse. Garrett sped around the end and into the open. Garrett raced all the way to

Miami's nine-yard line before being tackled.

"It was wide open," said Garrett. "All I had to do was take the ball and run. It was the perfect time to call it and it was perfectly executed."

Miami's "Killer Bees" did not give up. The Dolphin defense stopped Washington at the three-yard line. Moseley kicked a 20-yard field goal. Miami's lead was cut to a shaky 17-13.

The rest of the third quarter remained scoreless. Both teams failed to take advantage of opportunities. Miami linebacker A.J. Duhe intercepted a Theismann pass in Washington territory. But Woodley turned around and threw an interception of his own. Mark Murphy made a diving interception of Woodley's tipped bomb at Washington's four-yard line.

One play near the end of the third quarter summed up Miami's futility. Theismann dropped back to pass from deep in his own territory. Miami defensive end Kim Bokamper slammed in and blocked Theismann's pass. The ball floated straight into the air. Bokamper waited for the catch and easy touchdown. But, somehow, Theismann got in and knocked the ball down.

Miami carried its 17-13 lead into the fourth quarter. The Dolphins fought off Washington's next attack. Lyle Blackwood intercepted a Theismann pass at Miami's one-yard line.

But Miami's offense once again failed to move the ball. Washington took over at its own 48-yard line. And this time there was no stopping Big John Riggins of the Washington Redskins.

The Redskins faced fourth-and-one at Miami's 43-yard line. Gibbs signaled Theismann to go for it. The Redskins lined up with just over 10 minutes left in Super Bowl XVII. Theismann barked out the signals. Everyone knew what was coming. Theismann took the snap and handed off to John Riggins.

Riggins, who has marched to many drummers in his career, marched to the beat of greatness on this play. Miami's "Killer Bees" were wedged in tightly on the short yardage play. Riggins exploded through the left side of the line. He shed a last-ditch tackle attempt by defensive back Don McNeal. Legs churning, head down, ball clutched tightly, Big John Riggins swept down the field, through the end zone, and into the record books.

The Redskins mobbed the giant fullback. With 10:01 left in Super Bowl XVII, Washington led for the first time. Mark Moseley's kick gave the 'Skins a 20-17 lead.

Riggins' TD run was the longest in Super Bowl history. And it gave the Redskins an emotional edge they would never let go. The defense forced Miami to run three plays and then punt. The Redskins got the ball back at Miami's 41-yard line. The clock read 8:42, fourth quarter.

From there it was all John Riggins . . . Riggins to the left, Riggins to the right, Riggins up the middle. The Redskins chewed up the clock, chewed up Miami's proud "Killer Bees." With 1:55 left in the game, Theismann passed six yards to Charlie Brown for the insurance TD. The touchdown ended a 12-play, 6:47 drive, the longest drive in Super Bowl history. Moseley's kick gave the 'Skins a 27-17 advantage.

Miami's coach, Don Shula, brought in veteran quarterback Don Strock to rally the Dolphins. But the switch was too little and far too late. Strock fired three incomplete passes. The Redskins ran out the clock and claimed their first Super Bowl victory, 27-17.

John Riggins finished with a Super-Bowl record of 166 yards on a Super-Bowl record of 38 carries. Added to his Super Bowl record 43-yard touchdown run came the honor as Most Valuable Player of Super Bowl XVII.

"John Riggins was Mr. Universe," praised Dolphins' defensive end Doug Betters after the tough game. "Mr. All-Word. The MVP today. Their offense was no secret. Give it to John. They kept us off balance."

"John Riggins just did a good job finding his holes, and then he'd give it that extra surge and pick up another two or three yards," said nose tackle Bob Baumhower. "They have a good offensive line, but it's Riggins that makes it go."

"He was a dominant force," added Coach Don Shula.

The loneliest Dolphin in the lonely locker room was defensive back Don McNeal. He was the only Dolphin with even the slightest chance of stopping Riggins' run for glory.

"I was there," admitted McNeal. "I had the

position, but he's very physical, a tough guy to bring down. All your life they teach you to hit low, to stop the legs. The time came to do it, and I forgot what I had learned. Once I let go, I knew he was gone. I didn't want to get up."

"It's a play we ran all season," said MVP Riggins. "I told Joe [Theismann] that we were close to breaking it several times. I broke a tackle and got outside. I could go on about my speed, but no one would believe me."

Riggins' 166 rushing yards nearly edged Miami's entire offensive output for the day. The Dolphins managed only 176 total yards against the inspired Washington defense. And 76 of those yards came on the single TD pass play. The 'Skins pass defense held Woodley to 4 of 14 passing, including 0-for-8 in the second half. Washington's Theismann hit on 15 of 23 passes for 143 yards and two touchdowns. The 'Skins totaled 400 offensive yards against the respected "Killer Bees" of Miami.

"We did basically the same thing on defense we did all year with nothing different on our rush or our coverage," said 'Skins linebacker Monte Coleman. "We just had to play like Redskins."

"All year long, we have been holding people to the fewest points," said defensive tackle Dave Butz. "And today we showed how our defense can get after people. There was no question in my mind. All we have to do is hold them and give the ball to John Riggins. The guy is incredible."

Always the talk returned to Riggins.

"Before the game, I told the players that in the end, it would come down to physical toughness and John Riggins," said a smiling coach, Joe Gibbs, of the Washington Redskins. "And it did."

	1stQ	2ndQ	3rdQ	4thQ		Final
Miami	7	10	0	0	—	17
Wash	0	10	3	14	—	27

Miami — Cefalo 76 pass from Woodley (von Schamann kick)
Wash — FG Moseley 31
Miami — FG von Schamann 20
Wash — Garrett 4 pass from Theismann (Moseley kick)
Miami — Walker 98 kickoff return (von Schamann kick)
Wash — FG Moseley 20
Wash — Riggins 43 run (Moseley kick)
Wash — Brown 6 pass from Theismann (Moseley kick)

Attendance — 103,667

SUPER BOWL XVI

There was a new, fresh look to this sixteenth Super Bowl battle.

The location was a "first." The game was played in the Pontiac Silverdome, home of the Detroit Lions. Super Bowl XVI became the first Super Bowl to be played in a cold weather location. And the January afternoon *was* cold, too. The temperature fell below zero during the game. The wind chill factor lowered the temperature another 15 or 20 degrees. But inside the domed stadium the temperature rested at a comfortable 68 degrees.

The match-up was another "first." This was the first trip to the Super Bowl for *both* the San Francisco 49ers and the Cincinnati Bengals. First-timers hadn't met in a Super Bowl since Super Bowl IV. The Kansas City Chiefs and Minnesota Vikings were the newcomers then. So the Bengals and 49ers broke a string of 11 straight Super Bowls played by at least one repeater.

Both teams were filled with fresh, young players. Both teams had suffered through losing season after losing season until 1981. In 1981 the Bengals and 49ers surprised everyone by roaring through the regular season and into Super Bowl XVI.

Cincinnati posted an impressive 12-4 record during that incredible 1981 season. That was the best record in the American Football Conference. The Bengals easily won the championship of the tough AFC Central Division. Cincinnati edged Buffalo, 28-21, in the first round of the playoffs. The Bengals crushed San Diego, 27-7, in below-zero weather to win the AFC title.

San Francisco was even more impressive during the regular season. The 49ers won 12 of their last 13 games en route to a 13-3 record. That was the best record in the entire National Football League. One of those victories was over Cincinnati, 21-3, late in the season. The 49ers won the NFC Western Division title. They crushed the New York Giants, 38-24, in the first round of the playoffs. A stirring comeback led to a 28-27 victory over the Dallas Cowboys in the NFC championship game.

There was a fresh look to this sixteenth Super Bowl. The two teams with the best records in all of football were there. They were new teams, surprise teams. Their fans filled the Silverdome. Fans of the 49ers wore red and gold. Fans of the Bengals wore tiger stripes painted onto their faces. Some 81,000 fans packed the Silverdome. Hundreds of millions watched the game on television all over the world.

A lot of people had a feeling about this game. They had a feeling that Super Bowl XVI was going to be special, even for a Super Bowl.

The 49ers won the coin toss. They elected to receive. San Francisco didn't have the ball for very long.

Return back Amos Lawrence couldn't handle the kickoff. The ball bounced free. Cincinnati's John Simmons recovered the ball at San Francisco's 26-yard line. The Bengals had a huge break to start Super Bowl XVI.

A quick pass from Ken Anderson to Isaac Curtis moved the ball down to the 18. A pass to tight end Dan Ross moved Cincy down to the five. First down. A field goal seemed a certainty. But the Bengals wanted six. San Francisco's defense said "no way." The 49ers stopped Charles Alexander for no gain. Defensive end Jim Stuckey threw Anderson for a sack back to 11. On third down Anderson make a terrible mistake. He threw his pass right into the arms of 49ers safety Dwight Hicks. Hicks intercepted the pass at the five. He returned it 27 yards to his own 32.

The Bengals wasted their first opportunity. The 49ers were determined not to waste their chance. Quarterback Joe Montana started moving his offense down the field. A screen pass netted six yards. A short flare pass got six more. A Montana toss to wide receiver Freddie Solomon picked up nine yards. It was third-and-one. Most teams would have run their biggest back

The Detroit News Photo

The 49ers on a roll: a teammate runs interference for Earl Cooper, #49, ripping off yardage for San Francisco against Cincinnati.

up the middle. But not these exciting 49ers. They ran a little razzle-dazzle instead. Montana handed off to running back Ricky Patton. Patton handed off to wide receiver Freddie Solomon. Solomon faked the reverse and then pitched back to Montana. The strong-armed QB then hit tight end Charle Young on a big first down pass.

The fired-up 49ers drove right in for the score after the razzle-dazzle. Fullback Earl Cooper busted for 10 yards. Running back Bill Ring popped for six. Montana hit Young with a pass. Young was dropped at the one-yard line. Montana sneaked across for the first touchdown of Super Bowl XVI. Ray Wersching's kick gave the 49ers a 7-0 lead with 5:52 left in the first quarter.

Cincinnati got its next important drive rolling early in the second period. Anderson hit rookie receiver Cris Collinsworth with an 18-yard pass down to San Fran's 28. A couple of plays later Anderson hit Collinsworth again. Collinsworth was blasted at the five-yard line by defensive back Eric Wright. Wright's hard hit jarred the football loose. Collinsworth and cornerback Lynn Thomas scrambled for the ball. Thomas came up with the fumble at the eight. The Bengals had once more thrown away a scoring chance.

Montana again took advantage of the break. He directed his offense on an incredible 12-play, 92-yard scoring drive. Montana mixed up runs by his backs with short passes. The 49ers slowly ate up the field. Montana hit Young for a

20-yard gain. Montana passed to Dwight Clark for 11 more. A late hit penalty moved the ball down to Cincinnati's 10-yard line.

From the 10 Montana sent fullback Cooper on a delayed pass pattern out in the left flat. Somehow Cooper came wide open. Montana lofted a soft pass to the big back. Cooper grabbed the pass and rumbled into the end zone. Wersching's kick gave the 49ers a 14-0 lead with 6:53 left in the half.

The 92-yard drive by the 49ers was the longest in Super Bowl history.

The Bengals failed to move on their next drive. The 49ers started moving again from their own 34-yard line. Montana hit Clark for a quick 17 yards. Patton knocked off 10 yards on back-to-back carries. Short passes to Cooper and Clark put the ball down at the Cincinnati 20-yard line. Less than a minute was left in the half. Montana and Young hooked up on a pass play down to the five. The drive stalled there. Wersching kicked a 22-yard field goal. With 15 seconds left in the half, San Francisco had a 17-0 lead.

But the 49ers weren't finished yet. Wersching squibbed his kickoff across the artificial turf. Bengal after Bengal tried to grab the madly bouncing ball. San Francisco's Milt McCall finally pounced on the fumble down at the Cincinnati five-yard line. Ray Wersching kicked the 27-yard field goal. There were two seconds left in the half. The 49ers had a 20-0 lead in Super Bowl XVI.

The 20-0 halftime lead was the biggest halftime lead in Super Bowl history. The odds were stacked against the Bengals. But there was no give-up in Coach Forrest Gregg's players.

"You may not believe this," said Cincy tight end Dan Ross. "But we weren't all that rattled at halftime."

"Twenty points isn't that much," Coach Bill Walsh reminded his 49ers at halftime. He added, "We knew we were playing a great team."

The Bengals were down. But they quickly proved they weren't out of it. Ken Anderson and his mates started their first drive of the second half at their own 17. From there Anderson directed an impressive 83-yard scoring drive. Pete Johnson and Charles Alexander did most of the work on the ground. Anderson hit wide receiver Steve Kreider on a big 19-yard play. A razzle-dazzle pitch and pass to Issac Curtis moved Cincy down to the 49er 23. A roughness penalty moved the ball to the 11. Three plays later Anderson scrambled up the middle for a five-yard TD run. Jim Breech booted the extra point. San Francisco's lead was cut to 20-7.

Cincinnati's defense came alive, too. Twice the Bengals held the 49ers without a first down. Cincy's offense got the ball back at midfield late in the third period. Once again Anderson drove the Bengal offense right down the field. The biggest offensive play in the drive was a 49-yard Anderson bomb to Collinsworth. The rookie receiver was dragged down at the San Francisco

15-yard line. Four plays later the Bengals had a first down at the 49er three-yard line.

What followed was an awe-inspiring goal-line stand by the San Francisco defense. Pete Johnson, the 250-pound Bengal fullback, bulled to the one on first down. On second down Johnson was hammered back to the two by linebacker Jack "Hacksaw" Reynolds. On third down Anderson tossed a little flare pass to Charles Alexander. Alexander caught the pass. Linebacker Danny Bunz, amazingly, caught Alexander. Bunz wrestled Alexander down at the one-yard line.

Fourth and one. *Everything* rode on the next play. Anderson handed off to Johnson. The giant back crashed into the line. There he was met by "Hacksaw" Reynolds, Bunz, Ronnie Lott, and Archie Reese. Johnson never even got close to the goal line. The 49er defenders did a victory dance off the field.

"I'm surprised every time I'm stopped," said Johnson. "This time I was stunned."

"We had to stop him or the water would get awful hot," said Reynolds.

"Those were four of the most beautiful plays I've ever seen," said 49er defensive end Fred Dean.

"I almost knocked myself out," said Reynolds.

"That was a Super Bowl play," said Reese. "That should be a *Sports Illustrated* cover picture 25 times."

The goal-line stand killed an important Bengal

drive. But Cincinnati was far from finished. The clock clicked into the fourth quarter. Cincinnati was down 20-7.

Anderson engineered another scoring drive early in the final period. He hit Collinsworth for 11. He hit tight end Dan Ross for 10. A pass interference penalty put the ball on the San Francisco 15. Anderson hit Ross again for 10. The final Anderson-Ross connection resulted in a five-yard TD play. Breech kicked the extra point. Cincinnati had closed the gap to 20-14 with 10:06 left in the game.

Montana and the 49er offense came back alive under the pressure. Montana hit Mike Wilson for a big 23-yard gain. Ricky Patton rambled for gains of eight, two, and eight yards. A sneak by Montana, a run by Cooper, and two short gainers by Patton set up a field goal try. Wersching was good on the 40-yard kick. The 49ers had some breathing room, 23-14. Only 5:25 remained in the game.

Cincinnati's next comeback try ended in a deadly mistake. Defensive back Eric Wright intercepted an Anderson pass at the Bengal 48 and returned it down to the 22. A smiling Wright cradled the football and ran off the field. He had just become the first rookie to intercept a pass in the Super Bowl.

Six plays later Wersching tried his fourth field goal. The 23-yard kick was good. San Francisco had a 26-14 lead with 1:57 remaining in the game.

But the Bengals still refused to quit. Anderson went to work from his own 26. He hit Isaac Curtis for 21 yards. He hit Ross for 15 and again for eight. He hit Collinsworth for nine. He hooked up with Kreider for 17 yards. From the 49er three-yard line Anderson passed to Ross for the touchdown. Breech's kick was good. The score was 26-21.

Sixteen seconds remained in Super Bowl XVI.

The Bengals tried an onside kick. Dwight Clark recovered the ball for San Francisco. The 49ers lined up for a final play. Montana took the snap and fell to the ground. There he was mobbed by teammates as the clock wound down to zero.

San Francisco 26, Cincinnati 21.

After 36 long years, the 49ers owned their first National Football League championship.

The victorious 49ers carried Coach Bill Walsh off the field.

Back in San Francisco, fans of the 49ers streamed into the streets and began an all-night party. The city's buses became frozen in the downtown mob. Fans climbed atop the buses and danced their victory celebration.

The 49er locker room was a riot of palm-slapping, hugging, and happy screaming. Quarterback Joe Montana learned he had been named Most Valuable Player of Super Bowl XVI. President Ronald Reagan called the locker room and congratulated the champions.

"We kind of did everything we wanted to in the first half," said MVP Montana. "We were very happy with the big lead, but it came very early in the game and it almost cost us. The key to this victory had to be our defense. We made mistakes and didn't move the ball well in the second half, and they bailed us out."

Montana completed 14 of 22 passes for 157 yards and one touchdown. He threw no interceptions. San Francisco's only turnover was the fumble on the game's opening kickoff. The Bengals, on the other hand, turned the ball over four times. Cincy lost two fumbles and Kenny Anderson gave up two interceptions. Those interceptions ruined Anderson's otherwise fine performance. He completed a Super Bowl Record of 25 of 34 passes for 300 yards and two touchdowns.

"You can't play a Super Bowl game and turn the ball over and think you're going to win," said Anderson in the quiet Cincy locker room.

"We lost, but we have a lot to be proud of," said Bengal Coach Forrest Gregg. "No one expected us to be there. They weren't picking us to finish past third in the division. This is a dedicated bunch. They'll feel bad for a while, but not long. They don't have to hang their heads down."

"The goal-line stand really helped," said Jack "Hacksaw" Reynolds in the winning locker room. "I think it was a real lift for us and a real downer for Cincinnati, probably their turning point in the game."

"Nobody has stopped us on that play all year," said Gregg of the fourth-and-one goal-line play. "In a situation like that, you give it to the strongest guy. The 49ers did a good job. They jammed things up. He (Pete Johnson) tried to go underneath, and it didn't go. I think they just stopped us."

"It helped a lot," said 49er defensive back Ronnie Lott of the goal-line stand.

"This is the ultimate game," said Montana. "I didn't do that much. I think it (the MVP award) should have gone to 'Hacksaw' and the defense."

"I thought we were doing something good in the second half," said Anderson. "But then we got down to the one-yard line and couldn't get it in."

"I'm disappointed. Sure I am," added Gregg.

"To walk out on that field is probably the best feeling you'll ever know in the world," finished Anderson. "And to walk off like we did is probably the worst. And all in the same day. They won and they get the credit."

"Cincinnati showed tremendous character, coming back in the second half," said Walsh, the winning coach. "We beat a terrific football team. It is a rare moment for me to work with such a great group of men and win a Super Bowl championship. It is the greatest moment of my life."

Walsh also raved about his MVP quarterback, Joe Montana.

"He will be *the* great quarterback of the future," said Walsh. "He is one of the coolest competitors of all time and he has just started. He'll be even better in the future."

"Defense put us over the top," added Walsh. "If I live to be 100, I'll never forget that goal-line stand."

"No one remembers losers," said Cincy tight end Dan Ross. Ross set a Super Bowl record with his 11 receptions. That was three better than the old mark. "What's the difference if you're second or 28th?"

"Unbelievable! Fantastic!" shouted 49er lineman Keith Fahnhorst.

"I got my dancing shoes on," said reserve fullback Johnny Davis. "It's a lifetime dream. The money's nice, but I'll spend that. The Super Bowl ring lasts forever."

	1stQ	2ndQ	3rdQ	4thQ		Final
San Francisco	7	13	0	6	—	26
Cincinnati	0	0	7	14	—	21

SF — Montana 1 run (Wersching kick)
SF — Cooper 11 pass from Montana (Wersching kick)
SF — FG Wersching 22
SF — FG Wersching 26
Cin — Anderson 5 run (Breech kick)
Cin — Ross 4 pass from Anderson (Breech kick)

SF — FG Wersching 40
SF — FG Wersching 23
Cin — Ross 3 pass from Anderson (Breech kick)

Attendance — 81,270

SUPER BOWL XV

Jim Plunkett almost quit football at the start of the 1980 NFL season. He had quarterbacked an excellent pre-season for the Oakland Raiders. He had performed much better than newcomer Dan Pastorini. But head coach Tom Flores named Pastorini the starter for opening day.

Plunkett, hurt and angry, demanded to be traded. If he wasn't traded, he said he'd quit. Coach Flores had a long talk with the veteran quarterback. He convinced Plunkett to stay on as Pastorini's back-up. Plunkett backed down on his "trade me or I quit" stand. He agreed to stay on with the Raiders.

In the fifth game of the season Pastorini went down with a broken leg. He was finished for the season. Plunkett stepped in. The Raiders had a dismal 2-3 record when Pastorini was hurt. Everyone figured that the Raiders were finished. Jim Plunkett disagreed. He led the Raiders to an amazing 11-5 regular season record. The Raiders surprised the football world by earning a "wild card" berth in the AFC playoffs.

But these surprises were only the beginning. The Raiders bombed Earl Campbell and the Houston Oilers, 27-7, in the wild card match.

Then the Raiders upset the Cleveland Browns, 14-12, in the semifinal playoff game. The Raiders exploded their biggest surprise by pulling out a 34-27 win over the San Diego Chargers in the AFC title game.

The Raiders surprised everyone by making it to Super Bowl XV. But there was little surprise that the Philadelphia Eagles would be there as the NFC champions. The Eagles had knocked on the door in 1978 and 1979. In 1980 they were ready.

Philadelphia ran up a 12-4 record during the 1980 regular season. One of those wins was by 10-7 over the Oakland Raiders. The Eagles blasted Minnesota, 31-16, in the first playoff game. In the NFC title match, Philly routed arch-rival Dallas, 20-7. As expected, the hot young Eagles advanced to Super Bowl XV.

Philadelphia was making its first Super Bowl appearance. Oakland had been there twice before. The Raiders were crushed by the Green Bay Packers, 33-14, in Super Bowl II. The Raiders blasted the Minnesota Vikings, 32-14, in Super Bowl XI.

The Oakland Raiders were considered the "bad guys" by football fans. The Raiders had a lot of players who had been traded off by other teams as "discipline problems." Even during Super Bowl week, defensive end John Matuszak missed an 11 p.m. bed check. He was out partying. He didn't get home to the hotel until 3 a.m. Matuszak was fined $1,000.

Even Raiders owner Al Davis was considered an outlaw. He threatened all year to move his team to Los Angeles. The other NFL owners wanted the Raiders to stay put. Al Davis was not the most popular guy in pro football circles.

The Philadelphia Eagles were the "good guys." Coach Dick Vermiel had the toughest training camp and strictest rules of any NFL coach. The team was well-trained and enthusiastic. The Eagles were ready for the Super Bowl.

Jim Plunkett was ready, too.

Over 75,000 screaming fans jammed the Louisiana Superdome in New Orleans. Nearly 100 million fans the world over watched on television. The Oakland Raiders and Philadelphia Eagles lined up to start Super Bowl XV.

The Eagles took the opening kickoff. The first play from scrimmage was a big success. Running back Wilbert Montgomery sliced through the Oakland defense for an eight-yard gain.

The third play was just as big a disaster. Quarterback Ron Jaworski angled a pass for tight end John Spagnola. Linebacker Rod Martin stepped in front of Spagnola and picked off the pass. Martin returned the interception to the Philly 30-yard line.

Seven plays later the Raiders were at the Philly two. Plunkett dropped back to pass. He scrambled right. Then he fired into the end zone. Wide receiver Cliff Branch made the grab. Touchdown, Raiders! Chris Bahr kicked the extra point. Oakland led, 7-0.

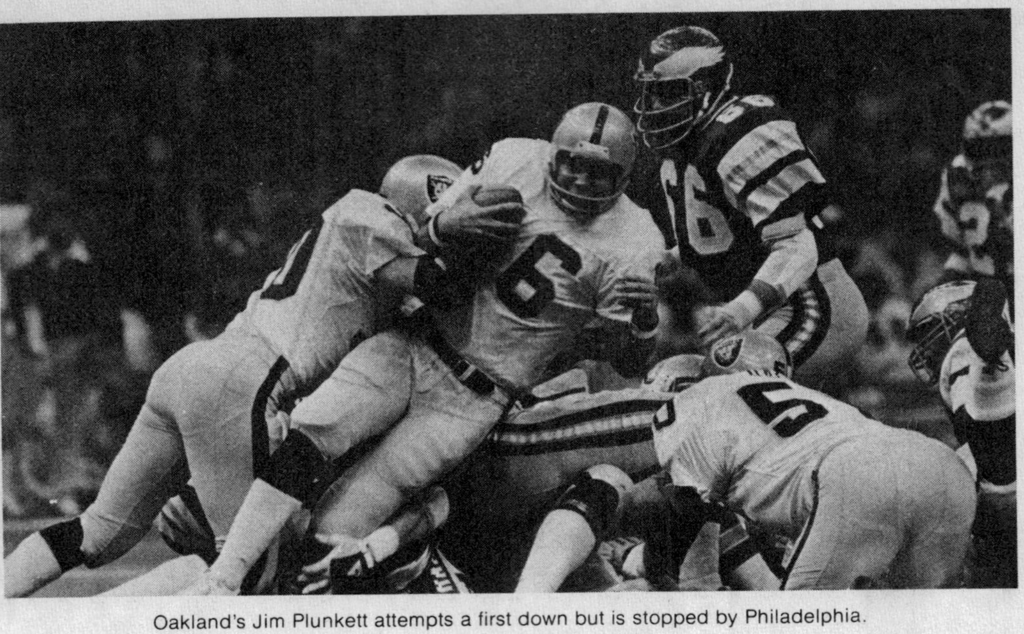

UPI Photo

Oakland's Jim Plunkett attempts a first down but is stopped by Philadelphia.

The Eagles came roaring back on their next drive. Ron Jaworski dropped back to pass from the Oakland 40. He scrambled. Then he fired a long one to wide receiver Rodney Parker. Parker made a great grab in the end zone. The Eagles began celebrating. But their joy didn't last long. A yellow flag rested on the turf. The touchdown was called back. Philly wide receiver Harold Carmichael had cut upfield too quickly. Illegal procedure. Philly lost five yards on the penalty. More importantly, they lost a touchdown and they lost momentum.

Oakland took quick advantage of the Philly flub. Plunkett set up to pass from his own 20. Again he was forced to scramble. Plunkett floated a pass to running back Kenny King. The ball dropped just over the outstretched arm of defensive back Herman Edwards. King made the catch near his own 35-yard line. He turned upfield and saw an open field ahead of him. The speedy back sprinted down the sidelines. No Eagle defender had a chance. King coasted into the end zone to finish out an 80-yard touchdown play. Bahr booted his second extra-point kick. Oakland led, 14-0. And the first quarter wasn't even over.

The pace of the game slowed some during the second period. Philly got its first score early in the period on a 30-yard field goal by barefoot kicker Tony Franklin. That cut Oakland's lead to 14-3. Halfway through the quarter Bahr missed a 45-yard field goal for the Raiders. The Eagles put together a solid drive near the end of the half. Franklin's 28-yard field goal try was kicked too low. Oakland linebacker Ted Hendricks blocked the kick. The half ended with Oakland up by 14-3.

Oakland put together another big drive in the third period. Plunkett set up for another long pass from the Philly 29. Once again he had to scramble. Plunkett fired deep to the left side. Defensive back Roynell Young jumped for the interception. But wide receiver Cliff Branch somehow cut in front of Young. Branch made a fine catch. Young grabbed Branch, but the speedy receiver lunged into the end zone. Touchdown, Oakland! Bahr's kick was perfect. The Raiders had a huge 21-3 lead.

The Raiders got another key break later in the third period. Linebacker Rod Martin picked off his second interception of a Jaworski pass. Plunkett drove the Raiders into Eagle territory. The drive stalled at the 29-yard line. Bahr cracked a 46-yard field goal. The third quarter ended with Oakland on top, 24-3.

The Eagles finally scored a touchdown early in the fourth quarter. An 88-yard drive ended with an eight-yard scoring pass from Jaworski to tight end Keith Krepfle. Franklin added the extra point kick. Philly closed the gap to 24-10. With some breaks the Eagles could get back into the game. Some 14 minutes remained in Super Bowl XV.

But the rest of the breaks belonged to the

Raiders. Oakland answered the Philly TD with a long offensive drive. Plunkett moved his team 72 yards to the Philly 18. From there Bahr kicked his second field goal, a 35-yard shot. Oakland upped its lead to 27-10.

Before the quarter was over, the Raiders had caused two more Philly turnovers. A Jaworski fumble was recovered by defensive end Willie Jones. Rod Martin sealed the Oakland victory by intercepting his third pass late in the game.

Super Bowl XV ended up a lopsided 27-10 for the Oakland Raiders. The Raiders thus became the first wild card team to ever win a Super Bowl.

The score was a lot more lopsided than the final stats. Oakland only outgained the Eagles 377 yards to 360. But the Eagles turned the ball over four times on three interceptions and a fumble. Oakland had no turnovers at all.

Jaworski completed 18 of 38 passes for a fine 291 yards. Wilbert Montgomery caught six of those passes for 91 yards. Harold Carmichael caught five for 83 yards. Montgomery led the Philly ground attack with 44 yards on 16 carries.

Mark van Eeghan led the Oakland rushers with 80 yards on 19 carries. Cliff Branch caught five passes for 67 yards. Bob Chandler picked up 77 yards on four catches. Plunkett completed 13 of 21 passes for 261 yards and three touchdowns.

Jim Plunkett, NFL Comeback Player of the Year, was named the Most Valuable Player for Super Bowl XV.

"I can't express my joy right now," said a choked-up Plunkett in the locker room after the victory.

"I knew we could win with Jim," said Oakland coach Tom Flores. "He is a good quarterback and we had confidence in him. When we reached the playoffs, I knew we could win. I knew we were as good as any team in the playoffs."

"This was our finest hour," said Al Davis, owner of the Raiders.

That "finest hour" included a number of Super Bowl records. The 80-yard touchdown pass from Plunkett to King was the longest in Super Bowl history. Rod Martin's three interceptions were the most by any player. Jaworski's 38 passes were the most by any Super Bowl quarterback. Jaworski and Plunkett combined for a record 551 passing yards. The six punts in Super Bowl XV were the least in history.

"I was running a simple six-yard out pattern when I saw Plunkett scramble," said King of his record-setting catch. "I took off up the field. The linebacker dropped me when he saw Plunkett scrambling. He got me the ball."

"We're the champs now," said Martin, his interception record nearly forgotten. "Nobody can deny us that."

"I can't say enough about Jim Plunkett," said big defensive tackle John Matuszak, speaking for all the Raiders.

And the guy almost quit football before the 1980 season!

The Philadelphia locker room was deathly quiet after the stunning defeat. The few players who had anything to say talked about mistakes. The Eagles made too many, the players agreed.

"I was surprised," said coach Dick Vermeil about all those mistakes. "I can't justify them. I thought we'd play better. But we didn't. When we gave Jim Plunkett pressure, he got off the big play. It's more than what we didn't do. It's what Jim Plunkett did to us."

"The Oakland Raiders deserved to win," said Vermeil. "They soundly beat us. They dominated us. The Oakland Raiders were a better football team."

And Jim Plunkett was the very best on a team of champions—the 1980 Oakland Raiders.

	1stQ	2ndQ	3rdQ	4thQ		Final
Oak	14	0	10	3	—	27
Phil	0	3	0	7	—	10

Oak — Branch 2 pass from Plunkett (Bahr kick)
Oak — King 80 pass from Plunkett (Bahr kick)
Phil — FG Franklin 30
Oak — Branch 29 pass from Plunkett (Bahr kick)
Oak — FG Bahr 46
Phil — Krepfle 8 pass from Jaworski (Franklin kick)
Oak — FG Bahr 35

Attendance — 75,500

SUPER BOWL XIV

Football fans and football experts agreed. The Los Angeles Rams didn't have a chance of winning Super Bowl XIV. Many jokes were told about the Rams in the week before the Super Bowl. The game was expected to be a "laugher." The Pittsburgh Steelers were planning to do the laughing.

In truth, the Rams did bring the worst record in Super Bowl history to the big game, 11-7. At one point in the regular season the Rams had a 5-6 mark. But the team won four of its last five games to finish at 9-7. That was a good enough record to win the National Football Conference Western Division.

The Rams opened the playoffs against the Dallas Cowboys. Dallas was the defending conference champion. The Cowboys had fallen to Pittsburgh in Super Bowl XIII. Dallas wanted a rematch. But Los Angeles quarterback Vince Ferragamo led his Rams to an upset victory. Ferragamo tossed three touchdown passes. Los Angeles whipped Dallas, 21-19.

The Rams met the Tampa Bay Buccaneers for the right to go to the Super Bowl. Frank

Corral kicked three field goals. The Rams won, 9-0. Not one touchdown was scored in the game. No championship game in NFL history had been without at least one touchdown. But the Rams didn't mind setting this record for bad offense. They were going to the Super Bowl for the very first time.

The Steelers made it to the Super Bowl in impressive fashion. Pittsburgh roared through a 12-4 regular season. The Steelers won the American Football Conference Central Division title. They opened the playoffs against the once-great Dolphins. It was no contest. Pittsburgh crushed Miami, 34-14.

Pittsburgh met the Houston Oilers in the AFC title game. The Oilers had finished 11-5 in the same division as the Steelers. The wild card Oilers made it to the title game on the incredible running of Earl Campbell. Pittsburgh routed Houston, 27-13, in the big match. The "Steel Curtain" defense held the mighty Campbell to just 15 yards on 17 carries.

So the Los Angeles Rams and Pittsburgh Steelers lined up for Super Bowl XIV. The Rams were in their first Super Bowl. For the Steelers it was Super Bowl number four. The Steelers were undefeated in the Super Bowl. Pittsburgh was favored by a solid 11 points. The Rams didn't have a chance, the experts said. So what if the Rams had beaten the Steelers in 10 of their last 11 meetings? This wasn't any old regular season game. This was the Super Bowl! Football fans warmed up their loudest laughs for use on the Rams after the big game.

Over 100,000 fans packed the Rose Bowl in Pasadena, California. Some 36 million people watched on television.

The game began as expected. The Steelers drove right down the field on their first possession. The Los Angeles defense finally stopped the Steelers at the L.A. 24-yard line. Matt Bahr kicked a 41-yard field goal. The Steelers led, 3-0, halfway through the first quarter.

Pittsburgh did a surprising thing on the kickoff. Bahr squibbed an onside kick toward the Rams. Los Angeles recovered the ball at the Ram 41-yard line. The Rams began their first possession with great field position. Ferragamo and his offensive mates wasted no time at all. Running back Wendell Tyler followed blockers Kent Hill and Dennis Harrah through a huge hole. The startled Steelers pulled Tyler down after a 39-yard gain. A couple of plays later running back Cullen Bryant blasted into the end zone from a yard out. Frank Corral booted the extra point. The already-surprising Rams led, 7-3.

"I was only inches away from breaking it all the way," said Tyler of the long run. "Their secondary is so fast they were all catching up with me. I slowed up to give some of the guys a chance to catch up and help out."

"That stunned us, confused us," said Pittsburgh all-star defensive tackle, "Mean Joe" Greene. "Nobody is supposed to run 39 yards on the

Steelers," Mean Joe added.

Pittsburgh didn't take long in striking back. Larry Anderson broke the kickoff for a 45-yard return. Quarterback Terry Bradshaw put together a perfect nine-play drive. Franco Harris took a pitchout around right end for a one-yard touchdown run. Matt Bahr added the extra point. The Steelers led, 10-7, early in the second quarter.

The Pittsburgh lead didn't discourage the Rams a bit. Los Angeles took the kickoff and drove right on down the field. The five-minute drive ended at the Pittsburgh 14. Frank Corral banged a 31-yard field goal. That knotted the score at 10-10.

Neither team threatened again until late in the second quarter. Terry Bradshaw fired a pass. Defensive back Dave Elmendorf intercepted the ball. Ferragamo directed a quick drive down to the Pittsburgh 28. Frank Corral boomed a 45-yard field goal with just 24 seconds left in the half.

The Rams went into the locker room with a 13-10 halftime lead. No one was laughing anymore.

"I was scared," admitted Pittsburgh linebacker Jack Lambert about the first half. "The Rams had the momentum going for them. I'm never concerned about our offense. But our defense wasn't playing well."

The Pittsburgh coaching staff decided to open up the offense in the third quarter. Bradshaw made a deep drop on the fifth play of the quarter. He fired a long pass toward wide

UPI Photo

Pittsburgh's Franco Harris plows through the Rams' defensive line on his way to a first down.

receiver Lynn Swann. Ram defenders Pat Thomas and Nolan Cromwell had Swann well covered. But Swann leaped high into the air and made an incredible catch. Swann came down at the two-yard line and ran into the end zone. The 47-yard TD pass and Bahr's kick gave the Steelers a 17-13 lead. Later that period Swann was knocked out on a six-yard pass play. He left the game with a concussion.

The Rams showed some of their own long ball offense during the next big drive. Ferragamo tossed a 50-yard bomb to wide receiver Billy Waddy. That set up the most surprising play of the game. From the Steeler 24, Ferragamo pitched wide to running back Lawrence McCutcheon. McCutcheon usually ran that play around end. Not this time. McCutcheon suddenly stopped, turned, and fired a pass into the end zone. Ron Smith made the catch on the halfback pass. Touchdown, Rams! Frank Corral's extra point kick sailed wide to the left. But that was OK with fans of the Rams. Their team led, 19-17.

"They were running that sweep all day and we got lulled with it," said Pitt cornerback J.T. Thomas about the surprise play. "We caught up with it, but they dropped it over our heads."

The quarter ended with Los Angeles leading, 19-17. The laughter was completely forgotten. The Steelers were now fighting for their lives.

Pittsburgh pulled off the longest play of the game early in the fourth quarter. Bradshaw dropped to pass from his own 27. He found wide receiver John Stallworth in the open. Bradshaw lofted the bomb. Stallworth cradled the ball at the Los Angeles 32. He sprinted into the end zone. The touchdown play covered 73 yards. Matt Bahr kicked the extra point. Suddenly the Steelers had the lead back, 24-19. The lead had already changed hands six times in this exciting Super Bowl match.

Ferragamo drove his troops on another long march. The Rams were at the Pittsburgh 32-yard line. A little over five minutes remained in the game. Plenty of time. Ferragamo faded back to pass. He fired deep. Linebacker Jack Lambert cut in front of the Ram receiver. He intercepted the pass at his own 14-yard line and returned it to the 30.

"It was the defensive play of the game," said Mean Joe Greene. "And Jack was the defensive player of the game."

"I don't think Ferragamo ever saw me," said Lambert.

"I saw Lambert at the last second," said Ferragamo.

The Lambert interception turned the game around. Bradshaw and his offensive partners made it count. Bradshaw hit Stallworth on a 45-yard pass play. Bradshaw fired a pass from the Ram 22 into the end zone. Defensive back Pat Thomas was called for pass interference. The ball was put down on the one-yard line. Franco Harris busted over for the TD. Bahr kicked his fourth extra point. Pittsburgh led, 31-19.

That's how Super Bowl XIV ended. The Steelers had their fourth Super Bowl victory. Pittsburgh became the "City of Champions." In one year the Pittsburgh Pirates won the World Series of baseball and the Steelers won football's Super Bowl.

The Rams lost by 12 points. That was a point more than the oddsmakers had guessed before the game. But no one was laughing at the Rams. Ferragamo, McCutcheon, Tyler, and the rest had helped make number XIV one of the top games in the history of the Super Bowl.

"They didn't outplay us," said L.A. Coach Ray Malavasi after the loss. "We ran on them. We threw on them. We just didn't get the big plays. I thought we were going to win right from the beginning and thought so right to the end. We're a good football team. We didn't get it this year, but we'll get our shot."

"I thought everybody played well," said Ferragamo. "We just weren't good enough to win. It's a bad feeling, but everybody's back next year and there'll be another Super Bowl game."

"We gave it our all," said defensive back Pat Thomas. "We felt that we should have won the game. The main thing that hurt us the most was a couple of big plays."

Ferragamo completed 15 of 25 passes for 212 yards. He tossed only one interception, the big one to Lambert. Billy Waddy led the Ram receivers with three catches for 75 yards. Tyler was the top runner for L.A. with 60 yards in 17 carries.

Pittsburgh's Bradshaw completed 14 of 21 passes. His 309 passing yards were only nine away from his own Super Bowl record. Bradshaw had two TD passes and three interceptions. Stallworth led the Pitt receivers with 121 yards on three catches. Franco Harris led the running attack with 20 carries, 46 yards, and two touchdowns. Franco's two TDs gave him a record four in his Super Bowl career. Bradshaw added to his Super Bowl career marks for passing yards (932) and TD passes (9).

There was very little surprise when Terry Bradshaw was named the Most Valuable Player in Super Bowl XIV. The MVP award included a huge trophy and a new sports car.

"I've never been so glad that a game's been over in my life," said Bradshaw after the battle. "The intensity and the buildup was so great that I stayed up all night last night.

"This was one of the toughest Super Bowls I've ever played," added Bradshaw. "They [the Rams] were really fired up. This victory has to be the best ever."

The happy Steelers were high in their praise of the Rams.

"They played practically a flawless game," said Pittsburgh head coach Chuck Noll. "They had no fumbles and their one interception came late in the game. They ran the ball well and Ferragamo threw the ball well."

"We didn't play well," said Mean Joe Greene. "The Rams played very tough—and we won anyway."

"We probably didn't think it would be as difficult as it turned out," admitted tight end Bennie Cunningham.

"It was a super win," said defensive back J.T. Thomas. It was especially super for Thomas. He had fought back from a rare blood disorder, missed a year of football, and returned at the top of his game. "There were none as good before us and none better to come after us."

NFL commissioner Pete Rozelle presented the Super Bowl trophy to Art Rooney, owner of the Steelers. Said Rozelle to Rooney: "You were tested by a fine Ram team and you kept coming back each time. I'm delighted to present this trophy to you for the fourth time. And I know you are especially proud to be able to again deliver it to your beloved city of Pittsburgh, the City of Champions."

There was a lot of laughter in the locker room of the Pittsburgh Steelers. But none of the laughter was directed at the losing Los Angeles Rams. The Steelers were just happy to get out of there alive—and with their fourth Super Bowl victory.

	1stQ	2ndQ	3rdQ	4thQ		Final
Los Angeles	7	6	6	0	—	19
Pittsburgh	3	7	7	14	—	31

Pitt — FG Bahr 41
LA — Bryant 1 run (Corral kick)
Pitt — Harris 1 run (Bahr kick)
LA — FG Corral 31
LA — FG Corral 45
Pitt — Swann 47 pass from Bradshaw (Bahr kick)
LA — Smith 24 pass from McCutcheon (kick failed)
Pitt — Stallworth 73 pass from Bradshaw (Bahr kick)
Pitt — Harris 1 run (Bahr kick)

Attendance — 103,985

SUPER BOWL XIII

Terry Bradshaw was ready. He and his Pittsburgh Steeler teammates were to meet the Dallas Cowboys in the biggest game of the year. Super Bowl XIII was the first rematch in the game's history. The Steelers had edged the Cowboys, 21-17, in Super Bowl X in Miami's Orange Bowl.

Super Bowl XIII was also to be played in the Orange Bowl. And Terry Bradshaw was ready.

"It's not any more meaningful this time around," Bradshaw said before his third Super Bowl. "Number three or things like that don't mean that much. I just want to win it because it's the Super Bowl."

Bradshaw had mentioned "number three." Both the Steelers and the Cowboys were shooting for their third Super Bowl triumph. Both teams wanted to be the first ever to win three Super Bowl games.

During 1978 Dallas had managed a 12-4 regular season record. The Cowboys nipped the Atlanta Falcons, 27-20, in the first round of the playoffs. Then Dallas blanked the Los Angeles Rams, 28-0, in the National Football Conference title game. That win earned the Cowboys their fifth Super Bowl trip in nine seasons.

The Steelers finished the season 14-2. That was the best record in the whole National Football League in 1978. In the opening round of the playoffs, Pittsburgh ran over the Denver Broncos, 33-10. The Broncos were the defending American Conference champions. The Steelers crushed the Houston Oilers, 34-5, to win the 1978 AFC title. Pittsburgh was on its way to the Super Bowl for the third time in five years.

Everyone expected Super Bowl XIII to be an exciting game. Many experts expected a lot of scoring. Pittsburgh's Bradshaw had thrown the most touchdown passes (28) in all of pro ball in 1978. Dallas' Roger Staubach had been rated number one in the league at quarterback.

The Cowboys and Steelers lined up for the start of Super Bowl XIII before 78,656 screaming fans in the Orange Bowl. The rain had stopped before kickoff. The field was damp but just right for football. Pittsburgh fans waved their "Terrible Towels" in the air. Dallas followers threw 10-gallon cowboy hats into the air.

The first break in the game went in favor of Pittsburgh. The Cowboys tried to set up a trick play. But Staubach and teammate Drew Pearson fumbled the handoff. Pittsburgh's John Banaszak recovered at the Steeler 34-yard line.

Bradshaw cranked up the Pittsburgh offense. He sent running backs Franco Harris and Rocky Bleier for short gains. He hit wide receiver John Stallworth and tight end Randy Grossman on passes for first downs. Then he faked the run and fired deep into the end zone. Stallworth was there. The receiver jumped, twisted, and made the catch. Touchdown, Pittsburgh! Roy Gerela kicked the extra point. The Steelers had a 7-0 lead in Super Bowl XIII.

The Cowboys got their first break late in the first quarter. Pittsburgh's Bradshaw set up to pass. He was smacked by Dallas defensive end Harvey Martin. The ball fell to the turf. Defensive end Ed "Too Tall" Jones recovered at the Pittsburgh 41-yard line. Two plays later Staubach fired a short pass to wide receiver Tony Hill on the left sideline. Hill caught the pass and raced all the way for a 39-yard touchdown. Rafael Septien kicked the extra point. The first quarter ended at 7-7.

The Dallas defense made things happen early in the second quarter. Bradshaw once again fell back to pass. He fumbled the ball, picked it up, and was hit by linebacker Tom "Hollywood" Henderson. Linebacker Mike Hegman jumped in and stripped the ball out of Bradshaw's hands. Hegman raced 37 yards with the stolen ball for an easy touchdown. Septien's kick was good. Dallas had a 14-7 lead.

The Steelers tied it up seconds later. Bradshaw dropped back to pass from his own 25-yard line. He hit Stallworth with a short pass on the right side. Stallworth slipped a tackle. The speedy receiver turned into the middle of the field. He

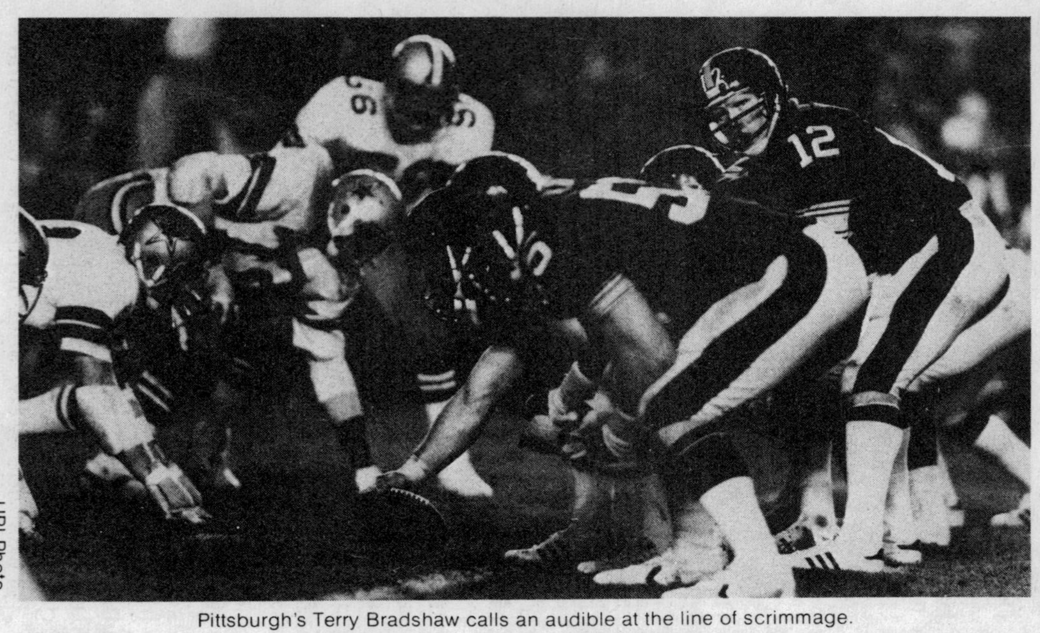

UPI Photo

Pittsburgh's Terry Bradshaw calls an audible at the line of scrimmage.

picked up blockers. He was gone! Stallworth went 75 yards for a touchdown on the short pass from Bradshaw. Gerela tied the game at 14-14 with his extra point.

Super Bowl XIII was already one of the most exciting Super Bowl games ever played. And it was less than half over.

Pittsburgh defensive back Mel Blount intercepted a Staubach pass late in the first half. Bradshaw started his offense moving from his own 45-yard line. Bradshaw tossed a flanker screen to Lynn Swann for a first down. He went back to Swann over the middle for another first down. Three plays later Bradshaw rolled to the right. He found Rocky Bleier in the end zone for a seven-yard touchdown pass play. Gerela kicked the point after touchdown. Pittsburgh had a 21-14 lead at halftime.

The Cowboys managed the only solid drive of the third period. Staubach mixed a short pass to Preston Pearson with runs by Tony Dorsett and Robert Newhouse. He moved Dallas to the Pittsburgh 10-yard line. On third-and-one, Staubach faked the run up the middle. Veteran tight end Jackie Smith sneaked into the end zone. Smith was wide open. Staubach lofted a soft pass to his receiver. Smith slipped, fell and the ball bounced off his hands. Smith slammed his hands angrily against the ground. The Cowboys had missed an easy chance at tying the game.

"I was wide open," said Smith after the game.

"There was absolutely no one near me. I was wide open and missed it."

"He feels as bad as I do," said Staubach. "Maybe I could have thrown a better pass."

The Cowboys settled for a 27-yard field goal by Septien. That made the score 21-17, the same score that had ended Super Bowl X.

The Pittsburgh offense got rolling again early in the fourth quarter. Bradshaw tossed a long pass from his own 43-yard line. The bomb was meant for Lynn Swann. Dallas defender Bennie Barnes and Swann tripped each other up. Barnes was charged with pass interference. The penalty gave the Steelers the ball at the Dallas 24-yard line. Two plays later Franco Harris banged loose up the middle for a 22-yard touchdown run. Gerela's extra point gave the Steelers a 28-17 lead.

Disaster struck the Cowboys on the kickoff that followed. Randy White fumbled the kick. Pittsburgh's Dennis Winston recovered on the Dallas 19-yard line. On the next play Bradshaw fired deep over the middle. Lynn Swann reached over his shoulders and hauled down the pass in the end zone. Touchdown! The Steelers had scored twice in just 19 seconds. Gerela's fifth extra point kick gave the Steelers a big 35-17 lead.

But the Cowboys did not give up. Staubach drove the Dallas offense right down the field. He completed five straight passes in an exciting 89-yard drive. Staubach hit tight end Billy Joe

DuPree in the right flat for a seven-yard touchdown pass. Septien's kick cut the Pittsburgh lead to 35-24.

On the kickoff the Cowboys tried an onside kick. Septien's kick bounced through the hands of a Pittsburgh player. Linebacker Dennis Thurman recovered for the Cowboys at the Dallas 47-yard line.

Staubach completed two passes each to Drew Pearson and Tony Dorsett as the Cowboys fought to come back. With 22 seconds left in the game Staubach tossed a four-yard touchdown strike to wide receiver Butch Johnson. Septien popped another extra point. Dallas had roared back. But the Cowboys were down 35-31 with time running out.

The Cowboys tried another onside kick. But Rocky Bleier of the Steelers grabbed the kick this time. Seconds later it was over. Super Bowl XIII ended at 35-31. The Pittsburgh Steelers had become the first team ever to win three Super Bowl games.

Football fans across the world were already calling it the greatest of all the Super Bowl games. Many records fell that day. The 66 points were the most ever scored in a Super Bowl game. The nine touchdowns and seven touchdown passes set new Super Bowl marks. Bradshaw set records for the most yards passing (318) and most touchdown passes (4) in a Super Bowl game. His 75-yard scoring pass to Stallworth tied the record. In Super Bowl V

Johnny Unitas passed 75 yards to John Mackey.

"Did I do all of that?" asked a happy Bradshaw in the locker room after the victory. The Pittsburgh quarterback had played his greatest game as a pro. For his record-setting performance he was named Most Valuable Player in Super Bowl XIII.

Bradshaw completed 17 of 30 passes. Stallworth caught three for 115 yards and two touchdowns. Swann caught seven for 124 yards and one touchdown. The Steelers put on the greatest passing show in Super Bowl history that day.

"We knew Bradshaw was the key and we didn't stop him the way we had to," said Dallas safety Cliff Harris. "They are really a good team, but Bradshaw made them great today. He deserved the MVP."

"I'm hurt that we lost," said a weeping Tom Henderson when it was over. "I'm hurt that I didn't make the big play to win the game."

The Cowboys did make a big effort. It just wasn't enough to come back and win. Quarterback Roger Staubach completed 17 of 30 passes for 228 yards. He threw three touchdown passes.

"I don't say Pittsburgh is better than we are," said Dallas coach Tom Landry. "But they were today."

"We were ready for them," said John Banaszak, whose fumble recovery set up the first Pittsburgh score. "I'm so happy. My career could end today and I'd go out with a smile."

"The two best teams in the NFL met today and the best team won," said Franco Harris. "We knew it would be a tough game and we were prepared. I think we'll be on top for a while."

Franco, of course, was right. Pittsburgh was on top in Superbowl XIV. But the excitement of Super Bowl XIII may never be matched. Many people still call it the greatest ever.

	1stQ	2ndQ	3rdQ	4thQ		Final
Pittsburgh	7	14	0	14	—	35
Dallas	7	7	3	14	—	31

Pitt — Stallworth 28 pass from Bradshaw (Gerela kick)
Dal — Hill 39 pass from Staubach (Septien kick)
Dal — Hegman 37 fumble recovery (Septien kick)
Pitt — Stallworth 75 pass from Bradshaw (Gerela kick)
Pitt — Bleier 7 pass from Bradshaw (Gerela kick)
Dal — FG Septien 27
Pitt — Harris 22 run (Gerela kick)
Pitt — Swann 19 pass from Bradshaw (Gerela kick)
Dal — Dupree 7 pass from Staubach (Septien kick)
Dal — Johnson 4 pass from Staubach (Septien kick)

Attendance — 78,656

SUPER BOWL XII

Before the start of Super Bowl XII, Craig Morton and Roger Staubach met at the middle of the field. The two quarterbacks hugged each other. Morton was in the uniform of the Denver Broncos. Staubach wore the colors of the Dallas Cowboys. They were about to battle it out for the football championship of the world.

Morton and Staubach had played together for the Cowboys for almost six seasons, from 1969-1974. They constantly fought it out for the number one quarterback spot. Morton was the quarterback in Super Bowl V. Staubach was the quarterback in Super Bowl VI.

Morton left the Cowboys in 1974. He played for two and a half years with the New York Giants. Before the 1977 season he joined the Broncos. He led Denver to a 12-2 regular season record. He led the Broncos past Pittsburgh in the first round of the playoffs. Then Morton helped Denver defeat the Oakland Raiders in the AFC title game.

"Roger the Dodger" Staubach led the Cowboys to a 12-2 regular season record in 1977. Staubach helped his mates to a pair of runaway victories in the NFC playoffs. The Cowboys destroyed Chicago and Minnesota on the way to the Super Bowl.

And so it was that the old friends—Morton and Staubach—were to do battle in Super Bowl XII. Unfortunately, only one of the veteran quarterbacks would end the day a champion.

Almost 76,400 excited fans turned out at the Superdome in New Orleans for the big game. Super Bowl XII matched two great quarterbacks. It matched a team in its first Super Bowl against a team in its fourth Super Bowl. It matched Denver's "Orange Crush" defense against Dallas' "Doomsday II" defense. Everyone expected a super Super Bowl game.

A super mistake by the Cowboys in the first few minutes of the game almost gave Denver a big edge. The Broncos punted deep. Dallas punt return ace Tony Hill took the punt near his own end zone. He fumbled the kick and there was a scramble for the ball. The Cowboys were lucky. Aaron Kyle recovered the ball at their own one yard line.

The "Orange Crush" stopped the Cowboys and Denver's offense got the ball. Morton faded back to pass. He was rushed by defenders Charley Waters and Randy White. Morton's pass was off target. It was intercepted by Randy Hughes at the Denver 25-yard line.

Staubauch took over and passed 13 yards to tight end Billy Joe DuPree. Running back Tony

UPI Photo

Dallas' defensive end Randy White hits the arm of Denver's quarterback Craig Morton. Morton's pass was intercepted by Dallas' Randy Hughes.

Dorsett ran for six yards. Then he ran for one yard. Dorsett got the ball again from the three. He ran off left tackle and scored standing up. Efrem Herrera kicked the extra point. Dallas led, 7-0.

Denver got the ball again. And disaster struck once again. Morton faded back to pass. He got a hard rush by defensive end Ed "Too Tall" Jones. Morton rushed his pass. It was tipped by linebacker Bob Breunig and intercepted by Aaron Kyle. Dallas had the ball at the Denver 35-yard line.

Staubach drove the Cowboys down to the Denver eight-yard line. There the "Orange Crush" defense held. Staubach threw one incomplete pass. Then he was sacked for an 11-yard loss. Herrera came in and kicked a 35-yard field goal. The Dallas lead was now 10-0.

The "Doomsday II" defense held the Denver offense once again. And the Broncos had to punt the ball back to the Cowboys. Dallas started its next drive from its own 43-yard line. Staubach passed to Preston Pearson for one first down. Bob Newhouse ran for another. The Cowboys drove to the Denver 25-yard line before the Broncos could hold the line. From there Herrera kicked a 43-yard field goal. The Dallas lead increased to 13-0. And it was still early in the second quarter.

Morton and the Denver offense continued to have problems. The frustrated Broncos lost three fumbles before halftime. One of those came when a Dallas punt hit a Denver player on the head. Morton tossed two more interceptions in the second quarter.

Morton had thrown only eight interceptions all season long. But in the first half of the Super Bowl XII he threw four interceptions. But the "Orange Crush" defense kept the game close. Denver lost the ball seven times on turnovers. But Dallas managed only 13 points.

The Broncos received the second half kickoff. They were hoping for a comeback. Morton finally got his offense moving. The Broncos moved down to the Dallas 30-yard line before running out of gas. Kicker Jim Turner popped a 47-yard field goal. The Dallas lead was cut to 13-3.

The Cowboys came back with a drive of their own late in the third quarter. The drive ended in spectacular fashion. Staubach sent wide receiver Butch Johnson on a long pattern. He stepped back and threw the bomb. Johnson beat the Denver defender and made a leaping, diving catch in the end zone. The incredible catch brought the crowd alive. Touchdown! Herrera added his second extra point kick. The Dallas lead was up to 20-3.

But the Broncos did not give up. Rick Upchurch received the kickoff following the touchdown. He took it at his own seven. Upchurch scrambled left, wiggled right, and streaked up the field. He was finally stopped at the Dallas 26-yard line. His 67-yard kickoff return was a Super Bowl record. The Broncos had their spirits up once again.

When the Denver offense took the field it was without Craig Morton. Coach Red Miller had decided to go with a younger, faster quarterback. So Norris Weese came in to lead the Broncos. He did a good job right away. It took Weese only four plays to lead Denver to a touchdown. Rob Lytle ran one yard for the score. Turner kicked the extra point. Denver had closed the gap to 20-10. And there was still plenty of time left.

The score stayed at 20-10 into the final period. Denver had the ball and hopes of a comeback. Weese faded back to pass. He was crushed by Dallas lineman Harvey Martin. Weese fumbled, and the Cowboys recovered at the Denver 29-yard line.

Dallas then delivered the killer. Staubach gave the ball to running back Robert Newhouse. He pretended he was running a sweep play. Suddenly, Newhouse stopped and threw a long pass. Golden Richards was down field. The pass was perfect. Richards caught the ball for a surprise 29-yard touchdown. Herrera added another extra point kick. The Dallas lead was 27-10.

Denver never got close to the end zone again. Super Bowl XII ended in favor of the Cowboys, 27-10. It was the second Super Bowl victory for Dallas against two losses. It was also the first Super Bowl win for the NFC after five straight AFC victories.

In the battle between the two old friends, Staubach had a big edge over Morton. "Roger the Dodger" completed 17 out of 25 passes for 183 yards and a touchdown. Morton threw 15 passes and completed four to each team. It was a rough day for Craig Morton.

"They just took away everything we had," said Morton in a quiet Denver locker room.

"They played well and we dropped the ball," said "Orange Crush" star Lyle Alzado. "You come this far and get into the championship game and blow it. I'm a little frustated. I am disappointed."

Spirits were high in the Dallas locker room. The "Doomsday II" defense had special reason to celebrate. Defensive tackle Harvey Martin and defensive end Randy White had just been named the Most Valuable Players in Super Bowl XII.

"We knew pressuring Craig (Morton) was the key, and it was all on our shoulders," said White. "We wanted it."

" 'Orange Crush' is soda water, baby," shouted a happy Martin. "You drink it. It doesn't win football games."

"This is very exciting," said Dallas Coach Tom Landry. "The Super Bowl is one of the greatest things in sports. This team has worked hard all year and they paid the price. They deserved it. Denver is a great team, and they could have come back at any time."

	1stQ	2ndQ	3rdQ	4thQ		Final
Dallas	10	3	7	7	—	27
Denver	0	0	10	0	—	10

Dal — Dorsett 3 Run (Herrera kick)
Dal — FG Herrera 35
Dal — FG Herrera 43
Den — FG Turner 47
Dal — Johnson 45 pass from Staubach (Herrera kick)
Den — Lytle 1 Run (Turner kick)
Dal — Richards 29 pass from Newhouse (Herrera kick)

Attendance — 76,400

SUPER BOWL XI

Fran Tarkenton had done it all in his 16 years of professional football. He was already considered one of the best quarterbacks ever to play the game. He had broken passing records held by some of the biggest names in National Football League history. He had helped his Minnesota Vikings to divisional title.

Tarkenton had done it all. Almost. There was one prize that Fran had not claimed. And that was the Super Bowl championship. The Vikings played in three of the first nine Super Bowl games. Tarkenton was the quarterback in two of those games. The Vikings lost every time.

Minnesota was set to try all over again in Super Bowl XI. The Vikings had run off an 11-2-1 record during the 1976 regular season. Minnestoa then crushed the Washington Redskins and edged the Los Angeles Rams to earn a fourth Super Bowl trip.

Fran Tarkenton had a lot to say before Super Bowl XI. The biggest boast of all came when he said, "I want the whole world to know that this time we are going to win the Super Bowl."

The Oakland Raiders, naturally, disagreed with Tarkenton. The Raiders also wanted their first Super Bowl victory. Oakland had played in Super Bowl II and had lost to the Green Bay Packers.

Oakland running back Pete Banaszak played on both Raider Super Bowl teams. "The last time we went to the Super Bowl, I was a little scared, to be honest about it," said Banaszak. "This time I'm not going to be scared. I know that Minnesota's good, because if they weren't, they wouldn't be here. And they're frustrated, too, like us, after being there three times without winning it. For one of the coaches, this is going to be a very big win, the biggest."

Oakland Coach John Madden had led his Raiders to a fine 13-1 regular season record in 1976. The Raiders then defeated New England and Pittsburgh in the playoffs.

Madden and Minnesota Coach Bud Grant met before 103,424 fans in Pasadena, California, for Super Bowl XI. Their Oakland Raiders and Minnesota Vikings were going to fight it out for the National Football League championship.

Tarkenton's Vikings got the first big break in the game. Late in the first period the Raiders were in a punt formation deep in their own territory. Minnesota linebacker Fred McNeill burst through the line. He jumped as Ray Guy put his foot into the ball. McNeill blocked the punt! It was the first Ray Guy punt that had ever been blocked by anyone. McNeill fell on the football at the Oakland three-yard line. It appeared the Vikings would score first in Super Bowl XI.

Minnesota running back Chuck Foreman got a yard up the middle on first down. Tarkenton handed off to running back Brent McClanahan on the next play. McClanahan ran into the line—and the football popped out. Oakland linebacker Willie Hall recovered the fumble at his own three-yard line. The Minnesota drive had ended. The score was still 0-0.

Quarterback Kenny Stabler ("The Snake") brought his Oakland offense to life after the recovery. Stabler directed a long drive that moved Oakland from its own three-yard line to the Minnesota seven-yard line. From there, Errol Mann kicked a 24-yard field goal. Oakland led, 3-0, early in the second quarter of Super Bowl XI.

Stabler put together a second scoring drive minutes later. "The Snake" sent running back Clarence Davis around left end for good yardage. He passed to tight end Dave Casper and wide receiver Fred Biletnikoff. The Raiders moved deep into Minnesota territory. Stabler fired a pass to Biletnikoff. Complete! Oakland was at the Minnesota one-yard line. Stabler lobbed a pass to Casper. Touchdown, Oakland! Errol Mann's extra point kick failed. Oakland's lead was up to 9-0.

The Raiders put together another big drive late in the first half. The running of Davis and receptions by Casper moved the ball down to the Minnesota 18-yard line. From there, "The Snake" faded back to pass. He threw the ball low to the ground. Bilitnikoff slid across the grass and made an incredible catch. Oakland had a first down at the Minnesota one-yard line. Banaszak, the veteran runner, blasted over for the touchdown. Mann's extra point was good this time. The Raiders had a huge 16-0 lead at halftime.

Tarkenton and the Vikes had played another disappointing first half of a Super Bowl game. In all four games the Vikings failed to score in the first half. The AFC opponents had a 51-0 halftime lead on the Vikings in the four Super Bowls.

But the Vikings came out smoking in the second half. Tarkenton and his mates felt they could make a comeback.

Oakland scored first in the third quarter. Stabler drove the Raider offense down to the Minnesota 23-yard line. From there, Mann kicked a 40-yard field goal. Oakland led, 19-0.

Tarkenton finally got his offense moving late in the third period. He threw short to Chuck Foreman and Sammy Johnson. He sent Forman for short gains on running plays. Tarkenton set up for a pass from the Oakland eight-yard line. He fired to rookie wide receiver Sammy White. Touchdown! Fred Cox kicked the extra point. Minnesota had cut the Oakland lead to 19-7.

The Vikings started another solid drive early

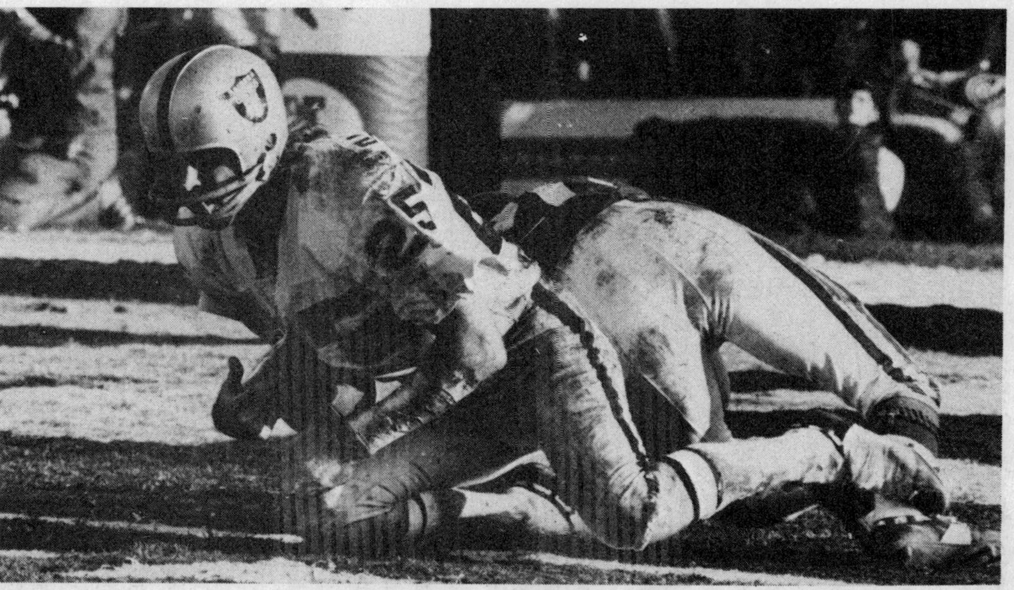

UPI Photo

Oakland's Fred Biletnikoff catches a Ken Stabler pass at the Minnesota one yard line.

in the fourth quarter. Tarkenton drove his offense from its own 22-yard line to the Minnesota 35-yard line. The Vikings were threatening to make the score closer still. Then Tarkenton threw a bad pass that was intercepted by linebacker Willie Hall.

"The Snake" Stabler went for the big play. He passed long to Biletnikoff down the middle. The play covered 35 yards. Banaszak crashed over from two yards out for his second touchdown. Mann was good on his extra point kick. Suddenly it was 26-7 in favor of the Raiders.

Tarkenton was forced to pass on every play. He made another bad pass. He threw into the zone of defensive back Willie Brown. Brown was one of four Raiders who played in the Super Bowl II loss. He was ready for Tarkenton's toss. He picked it off at his own 25-yard line. Brown, a 14-year pro veteran, returned the interception 75 yards for a spectacular touchdown. Mann missed another extra point kick. But it didn't matter much. Oakland had a 32-7 lead, and time was running out.

Bob Lee took over as quarterback for the Vikings. Tarkenton sat on the bench for the final minutes of Super Bowl XI. Lee moved the Vikings for a final score. He passed 13 yards to tight end Stu Voigt for the touchdown. Cox kicked the extra point. Lee's touchdown pass was too little, and it came too late. Super Bowl XI ended at Oakland 32, Minnesota 14.

The Vikings had lost their fourth Super Bowl

against zero victories. The Raiders had won their first after an earlier loss.

Oakland and Minnesota set 22 Super Bowl records in their 32-14 game. Most of the records involved the amount of yardage gained and points scored.

"We planned to wheel and deal, run and pass, throw short and deep and let everything go," said Raider Coach Madden after the victory. "After our first touchdown, Stabler came off the field and said, 'There's more where that came from.' "

Stabler hit on 12 of 19 passes for 180 yards. Casper and Biletnikoff each caught four passes. Biletnikoff's catches were so spectacular that he was named Most Valuable Player of Super Bowl XI.

Clarence Davis was another offensive star for the Raiders. He picked up 137 yards in just 16 rushing attempts. Running mate Mark van Eeghen gained another 73 yards in 18 carries.

The Vikings took the loss hard. "I'm disappointed because we may never be in another Super Bowl," said linebacker Jeff Siemon.

"They played extremely well," said Tarkenton. "And we played lousy."

"We shut them up by winning the big one," said Oakland linebacker Phil Villapiano.

"I still don't believe it," said Banaszak, the Minnesota veteran. "But I guess they can't take it away from us now. There's nobody else left to play."

	1stQ	2ndQ	3rdQ	4thQ		Final
Oakland	0	16	3	13	—	32
Minnesota	0	0	7	7	—	14

Oak — FG Mann 24
Oak — Casper 1 pass from Stabler (Mann kick)
Oak — Banaszak 1 run (kick failed)
Oak — FG Mann 40
Minn — S. White 8 pass from Tarkenton (Cox kick)
Oak — Banaszak 2 run (Mann kick)
Oak — Brown 75 interception return (kick failed)
Minn — Voigt 13 pass from Lee (Cox kick)

Attendance — 103,424

SUPER BOWL X

There was a lot of talk about "big plays" before Super Bowl X. This was highly unusual talk before a Super Bowl game. That's because so many of the previous games had had so few big plays. In fact, some folks were starting to call the game the "Boredom Bowl" instead.

But Super Bowl X brought together a pair of teams who liked to score points. True, the Pittsburgh Steelers and Dallas Cowboys had excellent defensive teams. But they also had dynamite offenses. Both teams could (and did) score from any spot on the field, at any time in the game.

"I don't know how it is going to turn out," said Pittsburgh Coach Chuck Noll. "It could go in either direction. Both teams have good, solid defenses, so it could be hard to control the ball. I think it might come down to the big play."

The big play had helped Pittsburgh to a 12-2 record for the 1975 regular season. The Steelers dropped the Baltimore Colts and Oakland Raiders on their way to the Super Bowl. This was Pittsburgh's second straight visit to the Super

Bowl. The Steelers were defending their National Football League championship.

Dallas had had a rougher road to the Super Bowl. The Cowboys finished 10-4 on the season and entered the playoffs as the wild card team. Dallas edged Minnesota and then slaughtered Los Angeles to earn a trip to the Super Bowl. The Cowboys thus became the first wild card team to make it to the big game.

Miami's Orange Bowl was packed with 80,187 fans for Super Bowl X. The weather was beautiful. And the big plays came early on, as expected.

Dallas made the first big play of the game. It happened in the first quarter. Pittsburgh punter Bobby Walden took the snap from the center. It was a good snap, but Walden fumbled the ball. The Cowboys recovered at the Pittsburgh 29-yard line.

Roger Staubach went right to work. He faked a handoff and went back to pass. He fired a strike to wide receiver Drew Pearson. Touchdown, Dallas! Toni Fritsch kicked the extra point. Dallas had the early lead, 7-0.

Pittsburgh wasted no time in coming back. The Steelers started their drive at the 33-yard line. Running backs Franco Harris and Rocky Bleier moved the ball to the Dallas 48-yard line. Then Terry Bradshaw fired a pass down the sidelines. Lynn Swann made an incredible catch and carried to the Dallas 15-yard line. Three plays later, Bradshaw fired a touchdown pass for seven yards to tight end Randy Grossman.

Roy Gerela kicked the extra point. The score was tied at 7-7.

Dallas drove for the only score of the second period, a 35-yard field goal by Fritsch. So the Cowboys led at halftime, 10-7

The Steelers had several chances to score during that second quarter. They came away with nothing. Gerela missed on field goal tries of 36 and 33 yards. One of those field goal attempts was set up by another big play. Again Lynn Swann was in on it. Bradshaw threw deep down the middle on the play. Swann made a diving, juggling, falling catch for a 53-yard gain.

The Dallas and Pittsburgh defensive units controlled the third quarter. Neither offense could move the ball. The score was still Dallas 10, Pittsburgh 7, at the start of the fourth period.

Dallas had to punt from its own four-yard line early in the fourth quarter. Mitch Hoopes took the snap and kicked the ball. But Reggie Harrison was right on top of Hoopes. Harrison blocked the kick, and the ball sailed out of the end zone. The safety gave Pittsburgh two points. And the score became 10-9, Dallas barely leading.

The Steelers received the free kick and started moving again. Bradshaw drove his offense down to the Dallas 19-yard line. There the Dallas defense held. Gerela kicked a 36-yard field goal. The Steelers had the lead for the first time in the game, 12-10. But there was a lot of time left.

Pittsburgh got another big play minutes later.

UPI Photo

Pittsburgh's Lynn Swann dives for a 53-yard gain.

Mike Wagner intercepted a Roger Staubach pass and returned the ball to the seven-yard line of the Cowboys. Again the Steelers were stopped by the Dallas defense. So Gerela was called upon for another field goal try. His 18-yard kick gave the Steelers a 15-10 lead.

Dallas failed to move on its next possession. The Steelers took over on their own 36-yard line. Bradshaw faked a handoff and faded back to pass. He threw the bomb. And there was Lynn Swann running under the ball. He caught it! Touchdown, Pittsburgh! The play covered 64 yards—another big play by Lynn Swann. Gerela missed the kick. But Pittsburgh had a 21-10 lead with 3:22 left in Super Bowl X.

But the Cowboys weren't dead. Roger Staubach drove the Dallas offense down the field. He found Percy Howard for a 34-yard touchdown pass. It was Howard's first and only catch as a professional football player. Fritsch made his extra point kick. Dallas had cut the lead to 21-17. And there was still 2:48 left in the game. It had taken Staubach only 34 seconds to drive for the touchdown.

The Steelers got the ball back. But the Dallas defense held fast. And Staubach brought his offense onto the field with 1:22 left in the game. There was still time.

Staubach drove his Cowboys down to the Pittsburgh 37-yard line. Dallas was threatening to take the lead. Staubach went back to pass. He fired the ball. Interception! Pittsburgh's Glen

Edwards picked off the pass to end the Dallas threat. He ran off the field waving the ball in the air. "We're number one!" screamed Pittsburgh fans.

Pittsburgh's 21-17 victory gave the Steelers two straight wins in the Super Bowl. Only Miami and Green Bay had done that before.

No one was surprised when Lynn Swann was named the Most Valuable Player in Super Bowl X. He caught four passes for 161 yards, a Super Bowl record. And every catch was spectacular.

"I caught none in the Super Bowl last year," said Swann in the loud Pittsburgh locker room. "I had to do something this year." He said of his 64-yard touchdown catch: "All I did was run under the ball."

"Lynn Swann was really something," said losing Coach Tom Landry. "He was the difference in the game."

Swann was the individual star. But it was the blocked punt that turned the game in Pittsburgh's favor. "The blocked punt changed the momentum," admitted Landry in the losers' locker room.

"There has been a lot about Super Bowls being dull," said Pittsburgh linebacker Jack Lambert. "Well, I think we gave fans something to be excited about in this one."

Fans had talked about "big plays" prior to Super Bowl X. After the game, that was all the players could talk about.

"A lot of times football games are won on big

plays," said Steeler running star Franco Harris. "We had the big plays today." Harris wasn't in on any of the big plays. But he worked hard all game long, carrying 27 times for 82 yards. Running mate Rocky Bleier had 51 yards in 15 carries.

"They had the big plays," agreed Dallas defensive star Jethro Pugh. "No doubt about it, you take them away, and it would have been totally different."

"We had our chances," said losing quarterback Staubach. "Overall, Pittsburgh is the best."

Pittsburgh turned out to be the best team in the best Super Bowl of the first ten games. Only one final score was closer. And none of the ten had as many big plays at all the right times.

The Pittsburgh offense received all the notice for the big plays. But Dallas wide receiver Drew Pearson had praise for the Pittsburgh defense. "They have the best defense we have played so far," he said. "There is no question. They just stand out. They shut everything down on us in the second half and got away from us."

Dallas tight end Jean Fugett sat in the locker room after the super loss and asked the right question. "Was it exciting?" he wondered. "I guess it was. I guess maybe we can't play a dull game."

And fans everywhere agreed that there was nothing dull about Super Bowl X.

	1stQ	2ndQ	3rdQ	4thQ		Final
Dallas	7	3	0	7	—	17
Pittsburgh	7	0	0	14	—	21

Dal — D. Pearson 29 pass from Staubach (Fritsch kick)
Pitt — Grossman 7 pass from Bradshaw (Gerela kick)
Dal — FG Fritsch 36
Pitt — Safety, Harrison blocked punt through end zone
Pitt — FG Gerela 36
Pitt — FG Gerela 18
Pitt — Swann 64 pass from Bradshaw (kick failed)
Dal — Howard 34 pass from Staubach (Fritsch kick)

Attendance — 80,187

SUPER BOWL IX

"Give me a D!" screamed the fans of the Pittsburgh Steelers.

"Give me a D!" shouted the fans of the Minnesota Vikings.

Fans for both teams yelled out "D" for "defense." Tulane Stadium was filled with 80,997 football fans. Nearly every one of them expected Super Bowl IX to be a battle of the defensive teams.

The Pittsburgh defense was nicknamed "The Steel Curtain." It had helped the Steelers to a 10-3-1 regular season record in 1974. "The Steel Curtain" shut down O. J. Simpson in the play-offs. It held Oakland's famous rushing attack to 29 yards in the AFC title game. "The Steel Curtain" was tough as nails. It had helped Pittsburgh to its first championship game in the 42-year history of the team.

Minnesota's defense had a nickname, too. "The Purple People Eaters" had led the Vikings to a 10-4 regular season record. Minnesota whipped St. Louis and edged Los Angeles in the playoffs. The Viking defenders put the club into its third Super Bowl game. The first two had ended in defeat. Minnesota wanted this one in a big way.

"Give me a D!" rang throughout New Orleans as the teams prepared for Super Bowl IX. "The Steel Curtain" and "The Purple People Eaters" were ready for the biggest football game of them all, the Super Bowl.

Super Bowl IX began in cold, windy weather in New Orleans. And it began perfectly for both defensive units. Neither offense could move the ball. The first quarter ended in a 0-0 tie. Football fans around the world wondered if either team would ever score a point.

The Steelers finally did score in the second quarter. But it was not the Pittsburgh offense that did the scoring.

Minnesota had the football at its own 10-yard line. Quarterback Fran Tarkenton faked a pitch-out. He then tried to hand off to running back Chuck Foreman. But the ball bounced off Foreman's hip. The ball rolled into the end zone. Tarkenton finally fell on it. And then a Steeler fell on Tarkenton. The safety gave the Steelers a 2-0 lead.

That was a wild play. But there was a wilder play in the first half. Tarkenton threw a pass. It was blocked by Pittsburgh defender L.C. Greenwood. The ball dropped right back into Tarkenton's hands. So Fran threw another pass and completed it to John Gilliam. But the officials called the play back. They said it was illegal to throw two passes on the same play.

"The Steel Curtain" stopped the Vikings cold during most of the first half. But late in the second period Minnesota got an offensive drive going. Tarkenton drove his team down to the Pittsburgh 25-yard line. Fran dropped back to pass. He fired long to Gilliam near the goal line. Gilliam reached for the pass. Defender Glen Edwards reached for Gilliam. The ball popped into the air. It was intercepted by Pittsburgh's Mel Blount. Minnesota's drive was finished. The half ended at 2-0 in favor of "The Steel Curtain." So far the fans were right. The two defensive teams were running the Super Bowl.

The second half began with another strange play. Pittsburgh kicker Roy Gerela slipped and fell as he kicked off. The ball bounced down the field. Minnesota's Bill Brown grabbed the ball. But he couldn't hold on to it. Pittsburgh's Marv Kellum recovered the fumble at the Minnesota 30-yard line. The Steelers had gotten a big break to start the second half.

Pittsburgh's offense finally got rolling. Running back Franco Harris began to turn it on. Harris ripped off 24 yards. The Steelers were inside the Minnesota 10. Quarterback Terry Bradshaw pitched again to Harris. Franco swept around left end. He rambled nine yards for the first touchdown of Super Bowl IX. Roy Gerela kicked the extra point. Pittsburgh led, 9-0. And that's how the third quarter ended. Minnesota's offense still couldn't get anything going.

The Vikings got their biggest break of the day

UPI Photo

Pittsburgh's Franco Harris looks for an open hole after receiving the ball from quarterback Terry Bradshaw.

early in the fourth quarter. Tarkenton threw a long pass to Gilliam. But Pittsburgh's Mike Wagner interfered with the Minnesota receiver. So the Vikings were given a first down at the Pittsburgh five-yard line. A touchdown would pull the Vikings to within two points of the Steelers. And there was a lot of time left in the game. But again "The Steel Curtain" did the job. Minnesota's Chuck Foreman carried from the five. He was smashed by "Mean Joe" Greene. Foreman fumbled the ball. And "Mean Joe" recovered it.

But "The Purple People Eaters" kept Minnesota in the game. The Steelers failed to move the ball after Greene's fumble recovery. Bobby Walden had to punt from deep in his own territory. Minnesota's Matt Blair raced through the line. Blair blocked Walden's punt. Terry Brown grabbed the ball in the end zone for a Minnesota touchdown. The extra point kick by Fred Cox hit the goal post and bounced away. But the Vikings had narrowed Pittsburgh's lead to 9-6 with over 10 minutes left in Super Bowl IX. Tulane Stadium was filled with excitement. The fans could feel the tension of a close game between two great football teams.

The Steelers started on offense from their own 34-yard line. Quarterback Bradshaw handed off to Franco Harris. He handed off to Rocky Bleier. He handed off to Harris again. And again. The Steelers drove down the field. Harris and Bleier ran for first down after first down. The clock wound down. The Vikings had to stop the Steelers. But Harris ran for another first down. Time was running out on the Vikings. Pittsburgh moved the ball down to the Minnesota four-yard line. There were less than four minutes left in the game. Bradshaw faked another running play. And then he tossed a short pass to tight end Larry Brown. Touchdown, Pittsburgh! Gerela's kick made it 16-6 with 3:31 left in the game. The Pittsburgh offense had moved 66 yards in 11 plays. They had used nearly seven minutes of valuable playing time.

The Vikings got the ball back. They were down by ten points and had barely three minutes of playing time. Fran Tarkenton went back to work. He threw deep, trying for a quick score. But Pittsburgh's Mike Wagner was right there. He intercepted the pass. Minnesota's chances got smaller.

The Vikings had one more chance with the football. But it was too, too late. And the Vikes were too far down. The final gun sounded on a 16-6 victory for the Pittsburgh Steelers. Super Bowl IX was history.

The Steelers had won their first National Football League title after 42 years of play. For the Vikings it was their third loss in three Super Bowl games.

Pittsburgh Coach Chuck Noll said after the game: "We came here with the idea of getting the job done. We did. It is especially fitting that on defense we shut out the champions of the

National Football Conference."

It was a victory for "The Steel Curtain." The Pittsburgh defense held the Vikings to a tiny 17 yards on 21 rushing attempts. Tarkenton had no better luck passing against the Steelers. He completed only 11 of 26 passes for 102 yards. He tossed three interceptions. Four of his passes were blocked. The Minnesota offense scored zero points in Super Bowl IX.

Pittsburgh's defense controlled the game. But it was an offensive player who took Most Valuable Player honors in Super Bowl IX. Running back Franco Harris earned the important award. He set two new Super Bowl records. He carried 34 times for an amazing 158 yards breaking Larry Csonka's 1974 record. The Steelers gained 249 yards rushing for the day. Bradshaw added 96 yards passing on nine completions in 14 attempts. Pittsburgh totaled 333 yards on offense.

"They were the best team today," said Tarkenton, the losing quarterback. "They deserved to win. We didn't. We did not take advantage of our opportunities. They did."

Bradshaw, the winning quarterback, drank champagne in the Pittsburgh locker room. "I've looked at all sides—being a hero and being a jerk," he said. "I think I can handle this well."

"I think it's O.K. for kids to idolize football players," said the idol of Super Bowl IX. "You need idols so you can day-dream."

"This is a big day," said Noll, the Steeler Coach. "We are going to enjoy it now for a very short time and then get ready for next year."

The Steelers—led by that tough "Steel Curtain"—had finally tasted victory. All they wanted after Super Bowl IX was to do it all over again next year.

	1stQ	2ndQ	3rdQ	4thQ		Final
Pittsburgh	0	2	7	7	—	16
Minnesota	0	0	0	6	—	6

Pitt — Safety, Tarkenton tackled in end zone
Pitt — Harris 9 run (Gerela kick)
Minn — Brown, fumble recovery in end zone (kick failed)
Pitt — L. Brown 4 pass from Bradshaw (Gerela kick)

Attendance — 80,997

SUPER BOWL VIII

Super Bowl VIII was more than just a big game for the young Dolphins from Miami. The Dolphins were playing for a place in the record books.

Only the Green Bay Packers had ever won two straight Super Bowl games. "The Pack" won the first two Super Bowls ever played. Those Packer teams were considered two of the best in National Football League history.

The Miami Dolphins wanted to join the Packers in the record books. The Dolphins already had a victory in Super Bowl VII. A triumph over the Minnesota Vikings in Super Bowl VIII would match the Green Bay record. Miami would then have to be called one of the best teams ever.

"We like to be talked of in terms of the Green Bay Packers," said Miami Coach Don Shula. His Dolphins had just defeated the Oakland Raiders in the AFC title game. "I can't be more proud of this team than I am right now."

Miami cruised to a 12-2 regular season record in 1973. The Dolphins crushed the Cincinnati Bengals, 34-16, in the first round of the playoffs.

Miami then smacked the Raiders, 27-10.

The Vikings were making their second Super Bowl appearance. Minnesota ran up a 12-2 regular season mark in 1973. The Vikes opened the playoffs with a 27-20 win over the Washington Redskins. Minnesota smashed Dallas, 27-10, in the NFC title game. That win put the Vikings in Super Bowl VIII against the Dolphins.

Super Bowl VIII was played on a chilly foggy day in Houston's Rice Stadium. Over 71,800 fans turned out for the game. They expected a battle between famous quarterbacks and famous defensive teams. Miami's Bob Griese and Minnesota's Fran Tarkenton were two of the best quarterbacks in the NFL. And Miami's "No Name Defense" joined Minnesota's "Purple People Eaters" as the toughest in the league.

The Dolphins took the opening kickoff in Super Bowl VIII. Miami started the drive at their own 38-yard line. The Miami offense rolled down the field. Griese handed off to full-back Larry Csonka. "The Zonk" crashed up the middle for good yardage on every carry. Griese mixed in a pair of passes with Csonka's driving runs. It took the Dolphins ten plays to move 62 yards down the field for the first score of the game. Csonka scored on a five-yard run straight up the middle. Garo Yepremian kicked the extra point. Miami led 7-0. The Vikings had yet to touch the football on offense. And the first quarter was over one-third finished already.

The Vikings took the kickoff. Tarkenton put

his offense into action. But Miami's "No Name Defense" held tight. The Vikes ran three plays and then punted the ball back to the Dolphins.

The Dolphins started from their 44-yard line this time. Griese handed off to Csonka. The big fullback ran for more tough yardage. Griese mixed in a couple of passes. And then he went to "The Zonk." The Dolphins worked their way down the field. They ate up hunks of time off the clock. Csonka rammed down to the one-yard line of the Vikings. Running back Jim Kiick smashed over for the touchdown. Yepremian added another extra point. Miami led, 14-0.

The first quarter was just about finished. The Dolphins had run 20 offensive plays. The Vikings had run only three. The score was lopsided already. Tarkenton and the Vikings faced a tough battle to come back in the Super Bowl.

Minnesota couldn't move the ball early in the second period. The Dolphins took over again. Griese once more got the Miami offense moving. The Dolphins moved close enough for Yepremian to try a field goal halfway through the second quarter. Garo's 28-yard kick was perfect. The Miami lead was up to 17-0.

The Vikings put together a solid drive near the end of the first half. Tarkenton put the ball into play from Miami's six-yard line. He handed off to running back Oscar Reed. The Miami defense smashed Reed. The ball popped loose. Miami recovered the fumble. The only Minnesota threat of the first half had been stopped by the Dolphins' "No Name Defense."

The half ended with Miami up by 17-0. Csonka and running mates Eugene "Mercury" Morris and Jim Kiick had eaten up good yardage in the half. Quarterback Griese had to throw only six passes the entire half. He completed five of them.

Minnesota opened the second half with a big play. John Gilliam received the Miami kick-off and took off on his return. Gilliam returned the kick-off 65 yards to the Miami 34-yard line. But a penalty brought the exciting play back. Minnesota had to start at its own 11-yard line instead of the Miami 34-yard line. The Vikings failed to move the ball. Miami's offense took over once more.

The Dolphins had only one drive in the third period. Griese's only pass of the second half came during this drive. The Dolphins were at the Minnesota 38-yard line. Griese fired a sideline pass to all-star wide receiver Paul Warfield. Warfield made an amazing diving catch of the pass. The play ended at the Minnesota 11-yard line. Several plays later it was Csonka once again. The big back busted over from two yards out for his second touchdown of the game. Yepremian kicked his third extra point. Miami increased its lead to 24-0. The Dolphins were moving closer to the record books.

The Minnesota offense finally got a good drive going early in the fourth quarter. Tarkenton moved his team down to the Miami four-yard

UPI Photo

Miami's quarterback Bob Griese watches the action after completing a pass to Paul Warfield.

line. He used short passes to Chuck Foreman and John Gilliam. He sent Foreman and Oscar Reed for short running gains. But it was Tarkenton himself who made the big play. Tarkenton ran in for the first Minnesota touchdown of Super Bowl VIII. Fred Cox kicked the extra point. Minnesota had cut Miami's edge to 24-7.

The Vikings tried an onside kick after the touchdown. Minnesota recovered the ball in Miami territory. But a penalty nullified the play. On the second kick try, Miami recovered the ball.

The Dolphins made it tough on the Vikings during the rest of the fourth quarter. Csonka kept banging for yardage and running down the clock. Punter Larry Seiple even helped bury the Vikes. Seiple kicked one ball that simply died at the Minnesota three-yard line.

The Vikings never managed to get out of the hole. Super Bowl VIII ended Miami 24, Minnesota 7.

"I am full of pride," said Miami's Shula after the biggest victory of them all.

"We played the way we are capable of playing," said Griese, the Miami quarterback. "We knew what we had to do to win, and we did it. And yes, this is a better team than last year. We achieved something we haven't before."

"I knew we were in trouble after their first drive," admitted Minnesota Coach Bud Grant. "They did the things that got them here (to the Super Bowl). We didn't."

Larry Csonka was the topic of much talk after the game. The big fullback carried the ball 33 times for 145 yards, both Super Bowl records. He scored two touchdowns. Csonka was named the Most Valuable Player of Super Bowl VIII.

"Mr. Csonka was not bad today," said Tarkenton, the losing quarterback. "He played as well as a fullback can. In all my years I've never seen any fullback play any better than he did."

While others talked of Csonka, he talked of his teammates. "I can't say enough about my offensive line," he said.

Csonka wasn't the only player to set Super Bowl records. Tarkenton completed a record 18 passes in 28 tries, good for 166 yards.

But in the end, Miami's "No Name Defense" stopped Tarkenton's offense cold. And Griese ran Csonka all over the field and into the record books.

So Miami joined Green Bay in pro football history. The Packers and Dolphins had each won two Super Bowl games in a row.

"You can certainly compare them," said Tarkenton, who had played against both great teams. "I've never seen the Dolphins play as well as they did today."

Some people later said that they had never seen *any* team play as well as the Dolphins did that day in Houston. They called those 1973 Miami Dolphins one of the greatest NFL teams of all time. And none of those Minnesota Vikings were about to disagree.

	1stQ	2ndQ	3rdQ	4thQ		Final
Miami	14	3	7	0	—	24
Minnesota	0	0	0	7	—	7

Miami — Csonka 5 run (Yepremian kick)
Miami — Kiick 1 run (Yepremian kick)
Miami — FG Yepremian 28
Miami — Csonka 2 run (Yepremian kick)
Minn — Tarkenton 4 run (Cox kick)

Attendance — 71,882

SUPER BOWL VII

Sixteen victories and no defeats. 16-0.

That's the record the Miami Dolphins brought into the Super Bowl VII. No team in pro football history had managed such a record before. No team had gone through the regular season undefeated. No team had won the league championship without losing at least one game. On record alone, the Miami Dolphins of 1972 were the best team in history. But they had to prove it by winning the Super Bowl.

Miami defeated the Cleveland Browns in the first round of the playoffs by 20-14. In the AFC title game, Miami edged the Pittsburgh Steelers, 21-17. That victory gave Miami a chance for the first 17-0 season in pro football history.

The Washington Redskins played the role of "spoiler" in Super Bowl VII. Fans throughout America wanted to see the Dolphins go all the way. The Redskins wanted to "spoil" it for them.

Washington had a solid 11-3 regular season record in 1972. The Redskins shut down the Green Bay Packers, 16-3, in the opening playoff game. Washington smashed the Dallas Cowboys,

26-3, in the NFC title game. The Cowboys were the defending Super Bowl champions. But it was Washington taking the trip this time around.

Miami had played in one Super Bowl game, losing to Dallas in Super Bowl VI. The Redskins had never before been in the championship game called the Super Bowl.

The Dolphins and Redskins were very different football teams. The Dolphins were young but cool and calm. Washington was a veteran team that played emotional football. Miami's defense was nicknamed "The No Name Defense." The Redskins were called "The Over-the-Hill Gang."

Miami quarterback Bob Griese was young. He threw a picture perfect spiral pass. Washington quarterback Billy Kilmer had played pro ball for a long time. His passes were called "wounded ducks" because they wobbled their way to receivers. But both quarterbacks were winners. They got the job done.

So it was that the Miami Dolphins and Washington Redskins met in Super Bowl VII. The game was played in Los Angeles, California, before 90,182 fans. On a hot, smoggy Sunday in January, Miami went after 17-0.

Defense controlled the early part of the big game. Miami's offense started a couple of drives. But penalties hurt, and the Dolphins turned the ball back to the 'Skins. Washington's offense couldn't get rolling. Manny Fernandez, Bill Stanfill, Nick Buoniconti, Mike Kolen, and the other Dolphin "No Names" were too tough.

Griese finally got the Miami running game moving late in the first quarter. Running backs Larry Csonka, Jim Kiick, and Eugene "Mercury" Morris all popped for short gainers. The Dolphins rolled to the Washington 28-yard line. Griese faked the run and faded back to pass. He found wide receiver Howard Twilley inside the 10-yard line. Twilley grabbed the pass at the five. He put a fake on defender Pat Fischer. Twilley ran into the end zone. Touchdown, Miami! Garo Yepremian kicked the extra point. There was one second left in the first quarter. Miami held a 7-0 edge.

Kilmer and the Redskins continued to have troubles with the Miami defense in the second quarter. But the Dolphins continued to drive for good yardage.

Early in the second quarter the Dolphins moved to the 47-yard line of the Redskins. Griese dropped back to pass. Speedy wide receiver Paul Warfield cut deep across the field. Griese lobbed the long bomb. Warfield ran under the pass, hauled it in, and went all the way for a touchdown. But there was a penalty flag on the play. The Dolphins were guilty. The play was called back. No one knew then just how important that touchdown would be later in the game.

The Redskins put a drive together late in the second quarter. Then Kilmer set up to pass from the Miami 48-yard line. Miami linebacker Doug Swift put pressure on the Washington quarterback. Kilmer threw a bad pass. Linebacker Nick

Buoniconti intercepted the ball at the Miami 41-yard line. He returned it all the way to the Washington 27-yard line.

Griese went right to work. From the 21-yard line he stood ready to pass. He found tight end Jim Mandich cutting across the field. Complete! Mandich made a diving catch at the two-yard line. Two plays later Jim Kiick ran the ball across the goal line from one yard out. Yepremian kicked his second extra point. Miami led, 14-0. There was less than one minute left in the first half.

Washington put together its best drive at the start of the second half. Kilmer threw short passes, and running back Larry Brown ran for short, tough yardage. The 'Skins finally stalled deep in Miami territory. Curt Knight was called on for a 32-yard field goal try. His kick was wide to the right. It was still 14-0.

The Miami offense ground out short yardage and ate up much of the clock in the third and fourth quarters. Both teams had scoring chances. Both quarterbacks threw interceptions into the end zone. The defenses were controlling the second half of Super Bowl VII.

Time was running out on the Redskins. The Dolphins were nearing the end of their 17-0 season. Griese drove the Dolphins into Washington territory with the clock running down to three minutes. The Dolphins moved close enough to try a field goal. Garo Yepremian came out to try a 42-yard boot for three points. A good field

UPI Photo

Miami's safety Jake Scott intercepts a pass thrown by Washington's Billy Kilmer.

goal would wrap it all up.

That's when disaster struck the Dolphins. Yepremian kicked the ball. It was blocked by the Redskins. The ball bounced back to Garo. He picked it up. He ran with it. He lifted it up to try a forward pass. The ball slipped out of Yepremian's hand. Washington's Mike Bass picked the ball out of the air. Bass ran all the way for a 49-yard touchdown. Knight added the extra point. Suddenly it was 14-7. There was time left for the Redskins to pull the upset.

Washington got the ball back with 74 seconds left in Super Bowl VII. The Redskins could not move against the "No Name Defense." Kilmer finally decided to try the long bomb, hoping for a miracle touchdown play. He went back to pass. His receivers went deep. The Miami defense climbed all over Kilmer. He went down hard. The ball never left his hand.

It was all over. Miami won Super Bowl VII, 14-7. The Dolphins were 17-0 for the season. And there was no one left to play. They had the best single season record in the history of the National Football League.

The Miami locker room was like a crazy house after the victory. Few of the Dolphins were happier than Coach Don Shula. He had already lost two Super Bowl games, one each as coach of the Baltimore Colts and the Dolphins.

"We won it for Shula," said Griese. "He lost two Super Bowls before. I'm happy for him."

Griese completed eight of only 11 passes for

88 yards. Most of Miami's offensive punch came on the running game. Csonka gained 112 yards in just 15 carries. Kiick added 38 yards and Morris had 34.

Miami's "No Name Defense" stole the show. Manny Fernandez seemed to be in on every Washington running play. Linebackers Swift, Kilen, and Buoniconti were all over the field. And the defensive backfield held Kilmer to just 14 completions in 28 pass attempts and just 104 passing yards. Safety Jake Scott intercepted two Kilmer passes, returning them 63 yards. Scott also broke up several passes and made a number of hard tackles. He was named the Most Valuable Player of Super Bowl VII.

"They're like swarming bees," said Washington guard John Wilbur about the Miami defense.

"They were the better ball club," said Washington Coach George Allen. "They deserved to win. They made fewer mistakes. We couldn't come up with the big play when we needed it."

Washington did get one big play. That was Yepremian's fumble that ended in the only Redskin score of the day. That play was the only black mark on a sparkling performance by the Dolphins.

"My mind went blank," said Garo after the mistake. "I was hoping Garo would just fall on the ball," said Shula. "I can guarantee you one thing. Yepremian will not be trying any more passes."

But every team in pro football will be trying to

match the accomplishment of those 1972 Miami Dolphins—a perfect 17-0 record.

	1stQ	2ndQ	3rdQ	4thQ		Final
Miami	7	7	0	0	—	14
Wash	0	0	0	7	—	7

Miami — Twilley 28 pass from Griese (Yepremian kick)
Miami — Kiick 1 run (Yepremian kick)
Wash — Bass 49 fumble return (Knight kick)

Attendance — 90,182

SUPER BOWL VI

The Miami Dolphins surprised everyone during the 1971 National Football League season. The Dolphins were less than five years old as a football team. Yet they raced through a 10-3-1 regular season.

Most people believed the Dolphins would get smashed in the playoffs. Wrong. Miami opened the playoffs with a 27-24 victory over the Kansas City Chiefs. It wasn't an easy victory. The Dolphins didn't win until the sixth quarter. That's right. Sixth quarter. Garo Yepremian's field goal ended the longest NFL game ever.

The Dolphins made a few more believers in the AFC title game. Miami beat the Baltimore Colts, 21-0. The Colts were the defending Super Bowl Champions. And the Dolphins shut them out.

So the Dolphins made it to Super Bowl VI as the AFC team. But still many people did not believe in Don Shula's team.

"It doesn't matter if anybody else believes," said Miami defensive tackle Manny Fernandez. "We believe."

On the other hand, everybody believed in the Dallas Cowboys. The Cowboys eased their way to an 11-3 regular season record in 1971. Dallas beat Minnesota, 20-12, in the first round of the playoffs. Then the Cowboys shut down the San Francisco 49ers, 14-3, to win the NFC title.

As expected, the Dallas Cowboys won a trip to Super Bowl VI. This was the second straight Super Bowl for the Cowboys. They had lost to the Colts in Super Bowl V. They wanted revenge.

So Super Bowl VI matched a team nobody believed in against a team everybody believed in. The Miami Dolphins and Dallas Cowboys lined up for the opening kickoff in Tulane Stadium in New Orleans. A sellout crowd of 80,591 braved the cold winds to see the final game of the pro football season.

The Dolphins made the first mistake in Super Bowl VI. Fullback Larry Csonka was carrying the football. "Zonk" had carried over 200 times during the regular season. And he had not fumbled the ball one time. But he did fumble the ball this time. Dallas linebacker Chuck Howley recovered the ball at his own 46-yard line. The fumble killed a good Miami drive.

Roger Staubach brought his Dallas offense into play. The Cowboys set the tone of the game during this drive. Running backs Duane Thomas and Walt Garrison pounded out yardage. Staubach tossed short passes to Thomas and Garrison and tight end Mike Ditka. The Dallas offense controlled the ball. Staubach drove the Cowboys down to the Miami two-yard line in 11 plays. There the drive stalled. Kicker Mike Clark was called into the game. He popped a nine-yard field goal. Dallas led, 3-0.

The young Dolphins faced a large task after the drive. Miami's defense had to stop the Dallas running game. And the Miami offense had to get its own running game going. The Cowboys were stopping Miami's famous running backs, Larry Csonka and Jim Kiick. "Butch Cassidy and the Sundance Kid" were getting nowhere against the Dallas "Doomsday" defense.

The Cowboys began their second drive in the second period. Thomas and Garrison continued to pound out big yards on the ground. Staubach continued to toss short passes. The Cowboys moved from their own 24-yard line to the Miami seven-yard line. From there Staubach stepped back to pass. He fired into the end zone. Veteran Lance Alworth was there. Touchdown! Mike Clark added the extra point. The Dallas lead was up to 10-0.

Miami quarterback Bob Griese got his Dolphins rolling late in the first half. Miami moved deep into Dallas territory. Griese dropped to pass. All-star wide receiver Paul Warfield was open across the middle. Griese fired. The ball was tipped. Warfield touched it, bobbled it, and dropped it at the two-yard line. The Dolphins missed a golden opportunity when Warfield missed the catch. The Dolphins settled for a 31-

UPI Photo

Dallas' Roger Staubach scrambles away from a Miami defender.

yard field goal by Garo Yepremian.

The first half ended Dallas 10, Miami 3.

Dallas took the second half kickoff. The Dolphins hoped their defense could hold. Then Griese and his offense could drive back to tie the game.

But the Miami defense wasn't up to the job. The Cowboys started the half at their own 29-yard line. The Dallas running game continued to grind out big hunks of yardage. Thomas and Garrison and Calvin Hill just couldn't be stopped. The Cowboys drove into Miami territory. Thomas rambled 23 yards to the Miami 22-yard line. Wide receiver Bob Hayes took a handoff on a reverse and sped 16 yards to the Miami six-yard line. Thomas crashed over from the three-yard line. Touchdown, Dallas. Clark added his second extra point. The Dallas edge was 17-3. The Dolphins were in a lot of trouble. But there was still lots of time in Super Bowl VI.

The Dolphins began to come back in the fourth quarter. Griese had the Dolphin offense moving behind runs by Csonka and Kiick and passes to Warfield. But the young Griese made a huge mistake. He tried to hit Kiick on a short pass over the middle. He didn't see linebacker Chuck Howley. Howley had been knocked down on a block. Howley got up just as Griese threw his pass. He cut in front of Kiick and made the interception. He picked up blockers and ran the ball down the field. Howley fell down at the Miami nine-yard line.

Howley later said that he fell down because he ran out of breath from running so far. "Please don't mention that," he asked of reporters. "I'm embarrassed." Embarrassed or not, Howley's interception broke up a good Miami drive.

The Dallas offense took over at the Miami nine-yard line. On the second play, Staubach set up to pass. He fired into the end zone to Mike Ditka. The tight end grabbed the pass for the third Dallas touchdown. Clark added another extra point. The Dallas advantage was up to 24-3. Miami was just about finished in Super Bowl VI.

The Dolphins got one more drive going late in the fourth quarter. But that drive also ended in a mistake. Griese fumbled a handoff to Csonka. Larry Cole recovered for the Cowboys.

Time was running out in Super Bowl VI. But the Cowboys started another offensive series after the fumble recovery. Dallas tried several trick plays during this drive. Dan Reeves ran the ball from a fake field goal set-up. Tight end Mike Ditka carried the ball on a reverse to the Miami one-yard line. But Calvin Hill fumbled on the next play. Manny Fernandez recovered for Miami.

Those trick plays made several Dolphins very angry. They felt the Cowboys were trying to run up the score. "They had us down and tried to kick sand in our face," said running back Eugene "Mercury" Morris.

Super Bowl VI ended in favor of the Dallas Cowboys, 24-3. The victory gave Dallas a 1-1 record in the Super Bowl.

"Winning the Super Bowl is everything an athlete wants," said Dallas quarterback Roger Staubach. "All the guys have tried and worked so long for this day. The way I see it was that in today's game my people were doing a lot of things right and maybe Griese's people were doing a lot of things wrong."

Staubauch completed 12 of 19 passes for 119 yards and two touchdowns. He also directed the Dallas running game to a Super Bowl record of 252 rushing yards. Duane Thomas led the runners with 95 yards. Walt Garrison had 74. For his leadership, Staubach was named the Most Valuable Player in Super Bowl VI.

"I am more happy for my team today than for myself," said Staubach after winning the award.

The surprising Miami Dolphins were disappointed with their play in the Super Bowl.

"We just didn't get the job done," said safety Dick Anderson.

"They came up with the big plays, and we didn't," said quarterback Bob Griese.

"They tore us apart defensively," said Coach Don Shula. "They completely dominated us. Dallas played near perfect ball. We were ready and we worked hard. But the only way you can prove it is to perform. We did not perform."

But Shula was happy that the young Dolphins had come so far in so short a time.

"We came a long way in two years, and I am very disappointed," he said. "The only way to make up for it is to win the Super Bowl another time."

While Shula looked to next year, Dallas Coach Tom Landry looked back at the Super Bowl victory.

"No one could stop us," he said. "We were all so determined to win."

Now, everyone had to believe in the world champion Dallas Cowboys.

	1stQ	2ndQ	3rdQ	4thQ		Final
Dallas	3	7	7	7	—	24
Miami	0	3	0	0	—	3

Dal — FG Clark 9
Dal — Alworth 7 pass from Staubach (Clark kick)
Miami — FG Yepremian 31
Dal — Thomas 3 run (Clark kick)
Dal — Ditka 7 pass from Staubach (Clark kick)

Attendance — 80,591

SUPER BOWL

The National Football League grew to 26 teams for the 1970 season. That was because the "merger" was completed. The ten teams of the American Football League merged with the 16 teams of the National Football League.

Two conferences were formed, the American Football Conference and the National Football Conference. Three of the 16 old NFL teams moved to the American Football Conference. The other 13 stayed in the National Football Conference. That way, the AFC and the NFC had 13 teams each. The three teams that moved to the AFC were the Pittsburgh Steelers, Cleveland Browns, and Baltimore Colts.

Super Bowl V was the first to match the winners of the AFC and the NFC.

The Baltimore Colts ran up an impressive 11-2-1 record in their first season in the new conference. The Colts blanked the Cincinnati Bengals, 17-0, in the first round of the playoffs. Then the Colts beat the Oakland Raiders, 27-17, to win the first AFC championship. And so the Colts, an old team in a new conference, went to the Super Bowl.

The Dallas Cowboys had a solid 10-4 regular season record in 1970. In the first playoff game, the Cowboys edged the Detroit Lions, 5-0. Dallas defeated the San Francisco 49ers, 17-10, in the NFC championship game.

The Dallas Cowboys traveled to Miami for their first Super Bowl game. Baltimore was making its second Super Bowl appearance. The Colts had lost in Super Bowl III.

Over 79,000 fans packed Miami's Orange Bowl Stadium for Super Bowl V. The day was sunny. The weather was perfect for football. Before the kickoff there was no hint that Super Bowl V would become known as the "Blunder Bowl."

The Baltimore Colts committed the first blunder of the game. In the opening quarter, quarterback Johnny Unitas set up to pass. He threw the ball, but it never got to a Baltimore receiver. Dallas linebacker Chuck Howley intercepted the ball. The Cowboys failed to score after the break.

The Colts were also guilty of the second blunder. Still in the first period, safety Ron Gardin went deep to receive a Dallas punt. He fielded the ball, put on a fancy move, and ran upfield. Only thing is, he left the ball back on the nine-yard line. Dallas recovered. Quarterback Craig Morton pushed the ball down to the Baltimore seven-yard line. From there Mike Clark chipped a 14-yard field goal. Thanks to a Baltimore mistake, Dallas had a 3-0 edge.

Morton led the Dallas offense on a good drive early in the second period. A Morton pass to Bob Hayes put the ball on the Baltimore six-yard line. Dallas took its turn to make a mistake. A penalty put the ball back to the 23-yard line. Instead of a short touchdown play, Dallas had to settle for another field goal try. Clark hit this one from 30 yards away. Dallas led, 6-0.

Baltimore cracked the scoreboard just minutes later on one of the strangest plays in Super Bowl history. Unitas fired a deep pass to wide receiver Eddie Hinton. The ball bounced off Hinton's hands. Then it seemed to brush the fingertips of Dallas cornerback Mel Renfro. And then the ball fell into the arms of Baltimore tight end John Mackey. Mackey caught the deflected pass at mid-field and ran untouched for a touchdown.

"Somebody touched the ball," agreed Renfro after the game. "I don't think I did." If Renfro had not touched the ball, the play would have been illegal. That's because two offensive players cannot touch a pass unless a defender touches it in between. But the referees ruled the play good. And Baltimore had tied the score, 6-6.

The score stayed tied, too. The Cowboys blocked the extra point kick by rookie Jim O'Brien. Everyone knew right away that the blocked kick was a big play in Super Bowl V.

The next Baltimore blunder ended in disaster for the Colts. Johnny Unitas fumbled the ball on a broken pass play. The Cowboys recovered at the Baltimore 28-yard line. Dallas quarterback Morton took over and drove his offense down to the seven-yard line. Morton threw a swing pass to running back Duane Thomas. Thomas ran it into the end zone for a touchdown. Mike Clark made his extra point kick. Dallas suddenly had a 13-6 lead.

The Colts made two more big mistakes in the first half. Unitas was smashed by Dallas defensive end George Andrie as he threw a pass. The ball fluttered downfield. Mel Renfro grabbed it off for the interception. But that wasn't the only bad news on the play. Unitas suffered a fractured rib on the hit by Andrie. He was finished for the day. So it was backup quarterback Earl Morrall who got to make the final Baltimore blunder of the half. Morrall moved the Colts down to the Dallas two-yard line with just seconds left in the half. Three running plays failed to get the touchdown. On fourth down, with 21 seconds left, Morrall tried to hit tight end Tom Mitchell. But the pass was incomplete. Dallas still held its 13-6 lead.

The Baltimore blunders continued in the third quarter. Jim Duncan took the second half kickoff for the Colts. He fumbled the ball. The Cowboys recovered at the Baltimore 31-yard line. Morton drove the Cowboys down to the Baltimore two-yard line. Morton handed off to running back Duane Thomas. Now it was Dallas' turn to make a mistake. Thomas fumbled the ball back to the Colts at the one foot line. Jim Duncan recovered the ball. The Thomas fumble was a key play in

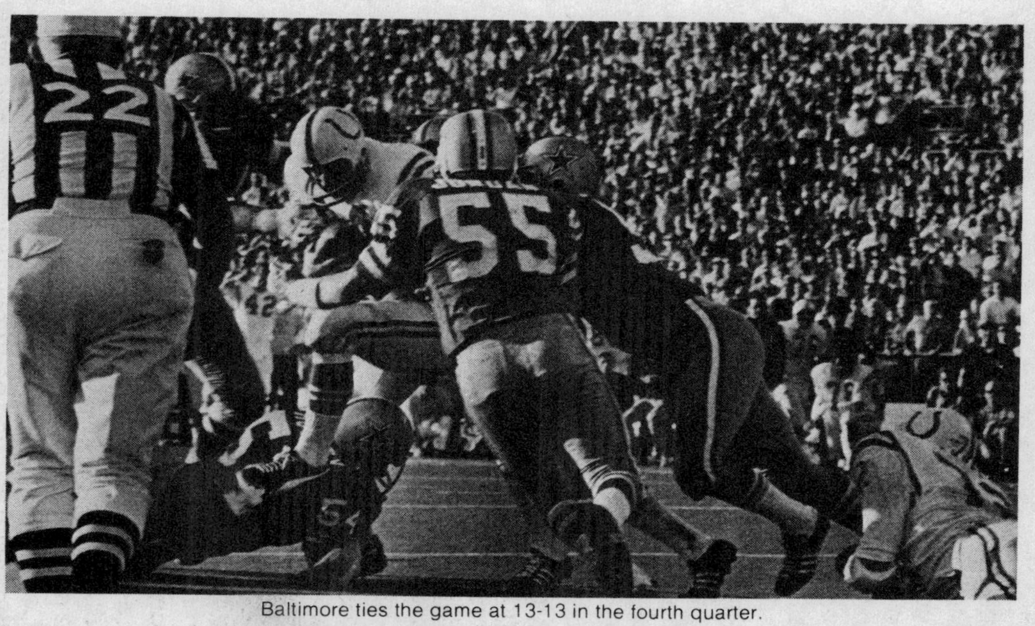

UPI Photo

Baltimore ties the game at 13-13 in the fourth quarter.

Super Bowl V. Had he scored, it would have been 20-6 for Dallas. But the blunder kept the Colts in the game.

The Colts made their final blunder early in the fourth quarter. That was when linebacker Chuck Howley intercepted another Baltimore pass.

Dallas took control of the blunders after that. Halfway through the final period, Morton passed to Walt Garrison. The ball bounced off his fingertips. Baltimore safety Rick Volk intercepted. He returned the ball to the Dallas three-yard line. Two plays later, Tom Nowatzke scored from the two-yard line. O'Brien's extra point kick was good this time. Super Bowl V was all tied up, 13-13.

Time was running out on the Colts and Cowboys. If the game ended in a tie, the teams would go into "Sudden Death." They would play until either team scored points on a touchdown, field goal or safety.

The Cowboys wanted to avoid going into "Sudden Death." And that's where Dallas made the biggest blunder of the "Blunder Bowl." There were less than two minutes left. Morton set up to pass. He fired the ball. Interception! Baltimore linebacker Mike Curtis picked off the pass and returned it to the Dallas 28-yard line.

Baltimore Coach Don McCafferty played it cool. He ordered Morrall to get off a couple of running plays and knock the clock down to less than ten seconds.

With the ball on the Dallas 25 and with nine

seconds on the clock, Morrall asked for a time out. The Baltimore field goal unit took the field. Every football fan in the world had his eyes on rookie kicker Jim O'Brien. They remembered that his first kick of the day had been blocked. The Cowboys wanted him to think about it, too. They called time out to shake up the rookie.

Finally, the teams lined up. Morrall took the snap from center Bill Curry. He put the ball point down on the ground. O'Brien stepped forward. He kicked the ball. The crowd went crazy. The ball sailed between the goal posts. The kick was good! The Colts had won Super Bowl V. The rookie had come through. The Baltimore players mobbed O'Brien. They had won, 16-13.

"I knew it was good when I hit it," said O'Brien with a big smile. "There was back-slapping and yelling, and we'd won. I hadn't thought much about being a hero in the game. Only of being a winner."

O'Brien's kick was one of the few plays that worked right in the "Blunder Bowl." The Colts gave up three interceptions, lost four fumbles and had a kick blocked. Dallas had three of its passes intercepted and lost that one important fumble on the Baltimore one foot line. Dallas Coach Tom Landry said that the fumble "was the big play of the game. From then on, it was all errors for us."

Dallas fans did have one victory to celebrate. Dallas linebacker Chuck Howley was named the Most Valuable Player in Super Bowl V. He was the first and only player from a losing team to win the MVP award.

"We beat ourselves," added Landry. "It was all there, and we lost it. I never thought we could lose."

Hero Jim O'Brien said, "I knew we'd either win or lose the game on a field goal." He was just glad that he did the kicking that helped his Baltimore Colts win the exciting "Blunder Bowl."

	1stQ	2ndQ	3rdQ	4thQ		Final
Baltimore	0	6	0	10	—	16
Dallas	3	10	0	0	—	13

Dallas — FG Clark 14
Dallas — FG Clark 30
Balt — Mackey 75 pass from Unitas (kick blocked)
Dallas — Thomas 7 pass from Morton (Clark kick)
Balt — Nowatzke 2 run (O'Brien kick)
Balt — FG O'Brien 32

Attendance — 79,204

SUPER BOWL IV

Super Bowl IV was to be the last Super Bowl for the American Football League. The ten AFL teams were going to join the 16 National Football League clubs for the 1970 season. After ten years of play the AFL would cease to exist.

Super Bowl IV was the last time for league champs to do battle for the biggest prize of them all.

The Kansas City Chiefs won the final American Football League title. The Chiefs had an 11-3 regular season record in 1969. Kansas City beat the New York Jets, 13-6, in the first round of the playoffs. The Chiefs then defeated the Oakland Raiders, 27-17, to win the AFL title.

Super Bowl IV was the second Super Bowl for the Chiefs. They had played, and lost, in the very first Super Bowl game.

The Minnesota Vikings ran up a 12-2 record during the 1969 regular season. The Vikings edged the Los Angeles Rams, 23-20, in the first round of the playoffs. Minnesota then beat the Cleveland Browns, 27-7, to win the NFL title and the ticket to the Super Bowl.

Minnesota and Kansas City both had excellent defenses. The Vikings were called the "Purple People Eaters." They were known for a rough-and-tough style of play. The Chiefs had no fancy nickname. But opponents found it awfully hard to score points against their speedy and strong defenders.

"I expect a close, fairly low-scoring game, because both of these teams have such good defenses," said Minnesota Coach Bud Grant before the game. Football experts thought Grant was giving the Chiefs too much credit. The Vikings were favored by 14 points over Kansas City.

Nearly 81,000 fans braved cloudy New Orleans weather and showed up for Super Bowl IV. Most of the fans expected the sun to shine on a Minnesota rout of the young Kansas City Chiefs.

As expected, defense controlled the early part of the game. Minnesota runners Bill Brown, Dave Osborn, and Oscar Reed were smacked down by Kansas City defenders. And when Viking quarterback Joe Kapp tried to pass, he was chased all over the field by Curly Culp, Aaron Brown, and big Buck Buchanan.

Kansas City runners Mike Garrett and Wendell Hayes were able to grind out short yardage. But early on, Chief quarterback Len Dawson was unable to generate much offense.

The Chiefs put together one short drive in the opening period. Dawson moved his offense to the Minnesota 41-yard line before the drive stalled. Jan Stenerud was called in to try a 48-yard field goal. The powerful kicker was good on his long attempt. The Super Bowl record field goal gave the Chiefs a 3-0 lead.

Kansas City again managed a short drive early in the second period. This time Dawson drove his club to the 25-yard line before losing steam. Stenerud kicked a 32-yard field goal this time. And Kansas City had a 6-0 lead in Super Bowl IV.

The Chiefs used a surprise play on their next possession to shock the Vikings. Dawson set up like he was going to pass the ball. Instead he handed it to wide receiver Frank Pitts on a reverse. Pitts rambled 19 yards with the ball. Again the Chiefs were deep in Minnesota territory. And again the "Purple People Eaters" stopped the drive. This time Stenerud attempted a 25-yard field goal. The kick was good. Kansas City had a 9-0 lead thanks to three field goals by Jan Stenerud.

The Vikings made a huge mistake on the kickoff which followed the field goal. Charlie West received the kickoff for Minnesota. He fumbled the ball. The Chiefs recovered at the Minnesota 19-yard line. Dawson took advantage of the error. He passed and ran his Chiefs down to the five-yard line of the Vikes. From there Dawson faked a sweep play and handed back to Mike Garrett up the middle. Garrett scored the first touchdown of the game. Stenerud added the extra point. Kansas City had a 16-0

UPI Photo

Kansas City's quarterback Len Dawson attempts to pass to his favorite receiver, Otis Taylor.

lead in Super Bowl IV. And the whole world was surprised at how easy it had looked so far.

The Vikings started the second half in a big way. Beginning at the Minnesota 31-yard line, quarterback Joe Kapp finally got the offense rolling. Brown and Osborn popped for short ground yards. Kapp fired passes to John Henderson and tight end John Beasley for important first downs. From the four-yard line of the Chiefs, Osborn crashed through the line for the first Minnesota score. Fred Cox kicked the extra point. The Vikings had closed the gap to 16-7.

But the Chiefs charged right back. Dawson moved his offense down the field. Pitts got a big first down on another tricky reverse play. Kansas City edged into Minnesota territory. From the Minnesota 46-yard line, Dawson fired a short pass to wide receiver Otis Taylor. Minnesota cornerback Earsell Mackbee smacked Taylor. But it was Mackbee who fell. And Taylor went racing down the field. The short pass turned into an exciting 46-yard touchdown play. Stenerud added his second extra point. Kansas City had a huge 23-7 lead.

Minnesota's Mackbee had to be helped from the field following the collision with Otis Taylor. "I pinched a nerve," he said after the game. "The arm went dead, and I couldn't grab him. That's how he got away."

The Vikings suffered an even bigger injury early in the fourth period. Quarterback Joe Kapp rolled out to avoid the Kansas City rush.

But defensive tackle Aaron Brown caught up with Kapp. Brown smashed Kapp to the ground. The Viking quarterback left the field holding an injured left arm. He was finished for the day.

Gary Cuozzo took over as quarterback for the Vikings. But he had no better luck against the fired-up Chiefs. The Vikings failed to threaten again in Super Bowl IV. The Kansas City defense stopped the Vikes on every play. And the Kansas City offense ran down the clock with running play after running play.

Super Bowl IV ended with a 23-7 Kansas City victory. The win gave the Chiefs a 1-1 record in the Super Bowl and the AFL a 2-2 record in the big game.

After the game, praise was split between Kansas City quarterback Len Dawson and the hard-hitting Kansas City defense.

Dawson completed 12 of 17 passes for 142 yards and one touchdown. He was named the Most Valuable Player of Super Bowl IV.

"We all wanted to get this one for Lennie Dawson," said defensive lineman Jerry Mays. "He's a fine gentleman and player. Lennie has had a lot of problems this year—his knee, the death of his father . . . "

"I'm particularly happy for Len Dawson," said Lamar Hunt, owner of the Chiefs. "I know how much this game meant to him."

The Kansas City defense held the Minnesota ground game to just 67 yards. Leading rusher Bill Brown had only 26 yards. Kapp managed to complete 16 of 25 passes for 183 yards against the Chiefs. But he was intercepted twice and sacked three times. Cuozzo added another interception in the fourth quarter.

"I don't know how much Kansas City hurt us and how much we hurt ourselves," said Minnesota defensive coach Jack Patera. "We got into the Super Bowl playing aggressive, but we couldn't—or wouldn't—be aggressive in this game."

The Kansas City pass defense was aggressive. "We knew they were long-ball conscious," said Chief cornerback Jim Marsalis, a rookie. "The movies showed us they like to go for the quick six, so our main concern was to cut that off." Marsalis and his mates succeeded. Kapp completed no long passes. And wide receiver Gene Washington was held to just one catch for only nine yards.

"We felt if we could outhit the Vikings, we could beat them," said Mays. "We were confident we were the better team."

"We played a great football team," said Minnesota Coach Bud Grant. "They beat us. It's as simple as that. I can say that Kansas City is the toughest team we've played this year. We put our best on the line. They put their best on the line. They were the better football team . . . today."

No one reminded Grant that he had predicted a close, low-scoring game. Grant had not expected his team to do the low scoring.

The Chiefs had two reasons to celebrate after the Super Bowl IV victory. They had earned revenge for the Super Bowl I defeat. And they had won the last Super Bowl for an AFL team.

"There definitely is a certain satisfaction in beating the National Football League," said Kansas City Coach Hank Stram. "We are proud champions of a proud league."

	1stQ	2ndQ	3rdQ	4thQ		Final
Kansas City	3	13	7	0	—	23
Minnesota	0	0	7	0	—	7

KC — FG Stenerud 48
KC — FG Stenerud 32
KC — FG Stenerud 25
KC — Garrett 5 run (Stenerud kick)
Minn — Osborn 4 run (Cox kick)
KC — Taylor 46 pass from Dawson (Stenerud kick)

Attendance — 80,562

SUPER BOWL III

Joe Namath did a lot of talking in the days before Super Bowl III was to be played in Miami.

The quarterback of the New York Jets made some comments about Baltimore Colts quarterback Earl Morrall.

"Earl Morrall would be third-string quarterback on the Jets," said Namath. "There are maybe five or six better quarterbacks than Morrall in the AFL."

That made some of the Colts angry.

"We're a better team than Baltimore," said Namath.

That made some of the Colts even angrier.

"I think we'll win it," said Namath. "In fact, I'll guarantee it."

That made some of the Colts angrier still. But it also made a lot of people laugh. After all, the Baltimore Colts were 18-point favorites over the New York Jets in Super Bowl III. Joe Namath might guarantee a New York victory, they chuckled, but the Colts were the better football team.

And so it went in the days before Super Bowl

III. Namath talked, and the football world listened. The first two Super Bowl games had not been very exciting. The Green Bay Packers slaughtered both American Football League opponents. At least Super Bowl III offered something of interest for the fans.

The New York Jets had scored an 11-3 record in the 1968 regular season. The Jets rallied from behind to beat the Oakland Raiders, 27-23, in the American Football League championship game. The Raiders had been looking for their second straight Super Bowl trip. But Namath and the Jets pulled out the victory and the tickets to Miami's Orange Bowl Stadium.

The Baltimore Colts had rambled to a fine 13-1 regular season mark. Their only loss had been to the Cleveland Browns. Baltimore beat Minnesota, 24-14, in the first round of the playoffs. The Colts met the Browns for the National Football League championship. Baltimore avenged its only loss of the season. The Colts clobbered the Browns, 34-0, to earn the right to meet the Jets in Super Bowl III.

Namath "guaranteed" a Super Bowl victory for the Jets. But New York Coach Weeb Ewbank tried to keep things under control. "I'm with Joe," said Ewbank. "But Baltimore is an established football team. We're green and growing. It depends on how the ball bounces."

"Everything we've accomplished this year as a football team goes on the line Sunday," said Baltimore Coach Don Shula. "If we blow it, everything is destroyed. We don't want everything to go down the drain. I'll be happy if we win convincingly and satisfied if we win."

The stage was set for Super Bowl III. Some 75,400 fans crowded into Miami's Orange Bowl on a cloudy Sunday in Jaunuary. The Baltimore Colts had Earl Morrall and the number one defense in the American Football League.

The Colts lived up to their reputation in the opening drive of the game. Runs by Tom Matte and Jerry Hill set up Morrall passes to Willie Richardson and John Mackey. The Colts drove to the New York 20-yard line before the Jets held defensively. Lou Michaels came in to try a 27-yard field goal. His kick missed.

The Colts continued to make key mistakes during the rest of the first half. Baltimore began one drive at the New York 12-yard line after a fumble recovery. Morrall threw an interception to Jet Randy Beverly in the end zone.

Later, running back Tom Matte broke through for a 58-yard run. Morrall followed with his second interception.

The Colts even wrecked a trick play with just 25 seconds left in the half. Morrall handed off to Tom Matte. Matte pitched the ball back to Morrall. Wide receiver Jimmy Orr was all alone in the end zone. Orr jumped up and down, waving his arms. But Morrall never saw him. Morrall fired down the middle instead. The pass was intercepted by Jim Hudson.

"I was the primary receiver," said Orr after the

game. "Earl said he just didn't see me. I was open from here (Miami) to Tampa."

Thanks to the interceptions, the Colts failed to score in the first half.

Namath took advantage of the Beverly end zone interception. He started his offense from the New York 20-yard line. Namath sent fullback Matt Snell time and again over offensive tackle Winston Hill. Hill cleared Colts Ordell Braase and Fred Miller from Snell's path. Snell knocked off five, six yards a crack. Namath mixed in passes with Snell's runs. "Broadway Joe" passed twice to wide receiver George Sauer, for 14 and 11 yards. He threw once to Snell for 12 yards. On the twelfth play of an 80-yard drive, Namath again handed off to Snell. The big fullback burst over from four yards out. Touchdown! Jim Turner kicked the extra point. The Jets had a 7-0 lead that stood through the first half of Super Bowl III.

The Colts continued to have problems early in the second half. On the first play of the third quarter, Tom Matte fumbled. The New York Jets recovered. Several plays later, Jim Turner kicked a 32-yard field goal. New York increased its lead to 10-0.

Namath started the New York offense moving midway through the third period. Snell continued to run through the Baltimore defense. And Namath was able to pop short passes to George Sauer, Bill Mathis, and tight end Pete Lammons. The Jet drive stalled at the Baltimore 23-yard

N.Y. Jets Photo

New York Jets' Joe Namath looks downfield for a receiver.

line. Jim Turner came on and kicked a 30-yard field goal. Turner's kick gave the Jets a 13-0 lead.

Baltimore Coach Don Shula sent in a new quarterback on the next Colt possession. Veteran Johnny Unitas replaced Earl Morrall late in the third period. Unitas had sat out most of the 1968 season because of arm troubles. But he entered Super Bowl III in hopes of picking up the Baltimore offense.

The Jets added their final score before Unitas was able to move the Colts. Jim Turner kicked his third field goal of the day early in the fourth quarter. His nine-yard kick gave the Jets a 16-0 lead.

Midway through the final period, Unitas started hitting his receivers. "Johnny U" completed four straight passes in putting together the best Baltimore drive of the game. Fullback Jerry Hill crashed into the line from the New York one yard marker. Hill scored the first Baltimore touchdown. Lou Michaels added the extra point. The New York lead was reduced to 16-7.

The Colts were successful on an onside kick. Unitas started another drive into New York territory. After completing three straight, Unitas threw three straight incompletions. The Baltimore drive stalled. It was all over for Unitas, Morrall, and the National Football League.

Joe Namath "guaranteed" the victory. Then Namath went out and won it. The Jets defeated the Colts by 16-7. The American Football League had won its first Super Bowl game.

"Do I regret what I said before the game?" asked Namath. "No, I meant every word of it. I never thought there was any question about our moving against their 'great' defense."

Namath completed 17 of 28 passes for 206 yards and no interceptions. He was named the Most Valuable Player of Super Bowl III.

Matt Snell finished with 121 yards in 30 carries. "Snell is a great runner," said tackle Winston Hill. "I knew we could do it. We ran against the best teams in our league. What's so special about the Colts?"

The New York offense played a great game, but so did the defensive unit. The Jets forced five turnovers and completely shut down the Baltimore passing attack. Morrall completed only six of 17 passes. Unitas hit on 11 of 24. Running back Tom Matte was the only bright spot on the Baltimore offense. He picked up 116 yards in only 11 carries.

"All week long all you read about was Joe Namath against the great Baltimore defense," said New York linebacker Larry Grantham. "Nobody wrote anything about our defense. But we felt that we had a chance to shut them out."

"They made the plays—we didn't," said Morrall. "It was one of those things. We didn't come up with the big plays."

"I don't think we did anything right," said Baltimore Coach Shula. "They deserved to win. When we finally did get going, it was too late."

It was too late for the Colts. And it was too late to save the National Football League. They could call it a fluke, but Joe Namath came through just like he promised. And the American Football League had shown it could play football as well as anyone else on the block.

	1stQ	2ndQ	3rdQ	4thQ		Final
New York	0	7	6	3	—	16
Baltimore	0	0	0	7	—	7

NY — Snell 4 run (Turner kick)
NY — FG Turner 32
NY — FG Turner 30
NY — FG Turner 9
Balt — Hill 1 run (Michaels kick)

Attendance — 75,389

SUPER BOWL II

The Green Bay Packers had been champions for a long, long time. Coach Vince Lombardi's "Pack" had won five National Football League titles in nine seasons. They had won the very first Super Bowl match. And there they were again, champs of the NFL, ready to compete in Super Bowl II.

The Packers had been winning championships long before the American Football League and the Oakland Raiders even existed. Some of the younger Raiders could remember swapping Bart Starr, Forrest Gregg, and Ray Nitschke football cards.

"It's like playing against your father," said one of the Raiders. "These guys were my childhood heroes."

"I'm looking forward very much to playing Green Bay," said Oakland quarterback Daryle Lamonica. "I was drafted by the Packers when I got out of college, but I chose the AFL. I think I would rather play Green Bay than any other team."

Oakland wide receiver Fred Biletnikoff said,

"We have to play our best. We know that. They're the champs."

The Raiders were champs, too. Oakland had romped through a 13-1 regular season record in 1967. In the American Football League title game the Raiders destroyed the Houston Oilers, 40-7. That win sent the Raiders to Super Bowl II with a fine 14-1 record.

The Packers had a so-so 9-4-1 regular season record in 1967. They beat the Los Angeles Rams, 28-17, in the first round of the NFL playoffs. The NFL title game was played in 13 degrees below zero weather in Wisconsin. The Dallas Cowboys held a 17-14 lead with time running out. On the last play of the game, Bart Starr kept the ball and dived over his offensive line. He barely got into the end zone for the winning touchdown. That Dallas-Green Bay game was called one of the greatest of all time. Some people wondered if the Packers could still get excited about another game.

"I never went into a game I didn't think I could win," said Coach Vince Lombardi. "I always go into every game scared and I go into this game scared."

Football experts didn't see any reason for the Packers to be afraid of the Oakland Raiders. Green Bay was a 14-point favorite to run away with Super Bowl II.

"They are favorites, I suppose, because they are a very fine football team with all the weapons and a fantastic record of success," said Oakland

Coach John Rauch. "Being the underdog makes you feel you've got to fight a little harder to win. We have been the underdog before."

"If we win, they'll say it's a fluke," said a hopeful Raider, receiver Ken Herock.

"I hope we don't get blown out of the ball park," said a less hopeful Raider, Coach John Rauch.

Super Bowl II matched the young Raiders against the veteran Packers. The game began before 75,546 fans in Miami's Orange Bowl. It was a warm and sunny day. Rumors spread before the game that Vince Lombardi was going to retire after the big game. That added even more excitement to Super Bowl II.

The Packers got their first possession at the Green Bay 34-yard line. Quarterback Bart Starr drove his offense right down the field. Runs by Ben Wilson and Donny Anderson and a 17-yard Starr pass to Carroll Dale moved the ball to the Oakland 32-yard line. From there Don Chandler chipped a 39-yard field goal. Green Bay had a 3-0 lead in the first quarter.

Green Bay started its next drive at its own three-yard line. Starr called the right play every time. Wilson and Anderson crashed through the line for short gains. Starr passed to Dale and tight end Marv Fleming. The Green Bay quarterback even ran 14 yards himself. This drive fell flat at the Oakland 13-yard line. Chandler popped a 20-yard field goal. Green Bay led, 6-0.

The Packer offense took over for the third

time. From the Green Bay 38, Starr dropped back to pass. He found Boyd Dowler wide open near midfield. Dowler grabbed it and ran all the way for a 62-yard touchdown. Chandler added the extra point kick. Green Bay's lead was 13-0. Super Bowl II began to look like a one-sided matchup.

But the Oakland offense came to life. Quarterback Daryle Lamonica got the ground game going. He sent backs Pete Banaszak and Hewritt Dixon off-tackle for good gains. From the Green Bay 23-yard line, Lamonica sent wide receiver Bill Miller into the end zone. Lamonica fired deep. Miller grabbed it. Touchdown! Veteran George Blanda kicked the extra point. Oakland had slashed the Green Bay lead to 13-7.

The Oakland defense finally stopped the Packers. Green Bay hit its first punt of the day. But Raider return man Rodger Bird fumbled the punt. Green Bay recovered near midfield. Starr put together a short drive. Chandler came on and kicked a long 43-yard field goal. Green Bay had a 16-7 edge at halftime.

Starr put together a long drive early in the third quarter. Good running plays by Wilson, Anderson, and Travis Williams gave Green Bay a third-and-one at the Packer 40-yard line. That's where Bart Starr pulled off one of his famous plays. Starr faked the run and threw deep downfield. Veteran Max McGee was there. McGee grabbed the pass for a 35-yard gain. Short passes to Anderson and Dale pushed the ball down to the Oakland two-yard line. Donny Anderson crashed over for the touchdown. Chandler added another extra point. Green Bay increased its lead to 23-7.

Minutes later Don Chandler added his third field goal of the game. His 31-yard kick gave the Packers a commanding 26-7 lead.

Early in the fourth quarter the Raiders buried themselves. Lamonica threw a pass deep into Green Bay coverage. Cornerback Herb Adderly intercepted the pass at his own 40-yard line. Adderly streaked towards the goal line. He picked up blocks from his defensive mates. Adderly went all the way for a 60-yard touchdown. Chandler kicked his third extra point. Green Bay enjoyed a 33-7 advantage.

Oakland struck for a final score late in the game. Lamonica passed to Bill Miller for another 23-yard touchdown play. Blanda added the extra point. Super Bowl II ended in a Green Bay romp, 33-14, over the AFC's Oakland Raiders.

Bart Starr was named the Most Valuable Player of Super Bowl II. He completed 13 of 24 passes for 202 yards and one touchdown. Starr directed a Green Bay offense that made no mistakes—no fumbles, no interceptions. Oakland made three turnovers and every one of them hurt.

"We weren't awed by their superman reputation," said Oakland Coach John Rauch after the loss. "We just made too many mistakes. But I was happy that at no point did we give up. That was the character of our boys all season. They are young and will get better."

Lamonica had a decent day passing against the powerful Packer defense. He completed 15 of 34 passes for 208 yards and two touchdowns. Of course, his one interception was a killer when Adderly returned it for six points.

"It wasn't our best effort," said Vince Lombardi after his second straight Super Bowl victory. "We're a good football team and we were ready for them."

"I know we did not play as well as we have," said Packer linebacker Lee Roy Caffey. "We made mistakes we don't make in most games."

Rumors of Lombardi's retirement continued after the game. But Lombardi wasn't talking about it. Some Green Bay players said that Lombardi himself was the reason they played so well.

"We decided we'd play the last 30 minutes for the old man," said offensive guard Jerry Kramer. "I wouldn't be surprised if Lombardi retires before too long, and all of us love him. We didn't want to let him down."

The Packers had routed two American Football League champions in the first two Super Bowl games. Many fans thought this proved that the AFL was still no match for the older National Football League. They thought it would be years before an AFL team would win the Super Bowl.

"They're getting better," said Packer defensive

tackle Henry Jordan. "If they improve as much each year, they'll be on a par with us soon."

"Oakland is a lot better than people thought," said offensive tackle Bob Skoronski. "Whatever the score was, we were in a tough ball game."

It may have been a tough game, but the Green Bay Packers were still world champions of the game of football. And Vince Lombardi would be able to retire knowing that he had done it all.

	1stQ	2ndQ	3rdQ	4thQ		Final
Green Bay	3	13	10	7	—	33
Oakland	0	7	0	7	—	14

GB — FG Chandler 39
GB — FG Chandler 20
GB — Dowler 62 pass from Starr (Chandler kick)
Oak — Miller 23 pass from Lamonica (Blanda kick)
GB — FG Chandler 43
GB — Anderson 2 run (Chandler kick)
GB — Adderly 60 interception return (Chandler kick)
Oak — Miller 23 pass from Lamonica (Blanda kick)

Attendance — 75,546

SUPER BOWL I

The Green Bay Packers and Kansas City Chiefs went through their warm-ups on the turf in the Los Angeles Coliseum.

The date was January 15, 1967, the first "Super Sunday" ever. Never before had teams from the National Football League and American Football League been on the same field at the same time. The Packers and Chiefs were going to do battle in Super Bowl I. They played not only for themselves but for the honor of their leagues.

The NFL was the old, established league. The AFL was only seven years old. The NFL had tried for years to ignore the young AFL. But the new league started signing the best college players. And the AFL started stealing veteran players from the old league. The NFL was forced to pay attention to the younger league. The NFL and AFL agreed to send their championship teams to meet in a season-ending football game. People started calling it the "Super Bowl." The name stuck.

"We're the kids from across the tracks," said

Kansas City lineman Jerry Mays. "We're coming over to play the rich kids."

The Packers were the richest of the NFL "rich kids." Under Coach Vince Lombardi, the Packers had won four NFL titles in the past eight years. In 1966, the Pack swept to a 12-2 regular season record. Green Bay won the NFL title by edging the Dallas Cowboys, 34-27, in a classic game. That earned Green Bay the Super Bowl trip. But it also put a lot of pressure on the Packers. The honor of the NFL went with Green Bay to the first Super Bowl.

"If we lose the game, the season won't mean anything," said Packer defensive back Tom Brown. "They will remember that the Green Bay Packers were the NFL team that lost to Kansas City in the first game played between the leagues."

Brown added: "A loss here would ruin all that Coach Lombardi has built up over the years. That thought haunts him, I'm sure, and it haunts us and drives us, too."

Guard Fuzzy Thurston said, "We want this one badly. We have worked for eight years to be the best. We just have to win to be considered the best."

Winning alone wasn't going to be enough for some of the Packers. "We have to show clearly just how big a difference there is between the two teams," said defender Lionel Aldridge. "One touchdown won't be enough."

Football experts figured it would be a lot more than one touchdown. Green Bay was favored by at least 14 points over the young Kansas City Chiefs.

"We want to play the best," said Kansas City's Mays. "The Packers are established as the best in the NFL over a period of years."

"We'll show them," said Packer defender Willie Wood. "The only thing that counts is combat, head to head, for 60 minutes on the field."

Only 61,946 fans turned out for Super Bowl I in the giant Los Angeles Coliseum. The Packers and Chiefs took the field on a warm, sunny day. They were about to make pro football history.

Green Bay got its offense going halfway through the first quarter. Quarterback Bart Starr moved his Packers down the field on runs by Jim Taylor and Elijah Pitts. From the Kansas City 37-yard line, Starr set up to pass. Starr threw deep to 34-year-old receiver Max McGee. The veteran pulled the ball into his chest and ran for the touchdown. Don Chandler kicked the extra point. Green Bay led 7-0 at the end of the first quarter.

Kansas City's offense made its move early in the second period. Quarterback Len Dawson found that short passes would work against the Green Bay defense. He hit Mike Garrett, Chris Burford, and Otis Taylor during a long drive. Dawson passed again from the Green Bay seven-yard line. He hit fullback Curtis McClinton. The big fullback carried the ball in for a touchdown. Mike Mercer kicked the extra point. The

UPI Photo

Green Bays' Bart Starr barks the signals in the very first Super Bowl game.

Chiefs surprised the football world by tying the score at 7-7.

The Packers struck right back on their next possession. Starr drove the Pack 73 yards in 13 plays for the go-ahead score. Fullback Jim Taylor scored the touchdown on a 14-yard power sweep. Linemen Bob Skoronski, Jerry Kramer, and Fuzzy Thurston led Taylor on the famous Green Bay play. Chandler kicked his second extra point. Green Bay led, 14-7.

The Green Bay lead might have been even bigger at this point. But a 64-yard touchdown pass from Starr to Carroll Dale was called back because of a penalty.

Late in the half, the Chiefs drove for more points. Dawson used his short passing offense to drive the Chiefs down to the Green Bay 24-yard line. Mike Mercer kicked a 31-yard field goal. Kansas City moved closer, 14-10, as the first half ended.

"We were a little too cautious in the first half," said Packer defensive end Willie Davis. "I figured, forget Kansas City and the Super Bowl and do what you do best."

The Packer defense took Davis' advice in the third quarter. Dawson was again moving the Chiefs with short passes. He faded back to pass again. The Packers sent two linebackers on a blitz. They pressured Dawson, and he threw a bad pass. Willie Wood intercepted at the Green Bay 45-yard line. He returned it all the way to the five-yard line of the Chiefs. On the next play, Elijah Pitts ran in for the touchdown. Chandler kicked the extra point. Green Bay held a 21-10 edge.

"We played well in the first half and got off to a good start in the second half," said Kansas City Coach Hank Stram. "We were doing the things we do well. Then the interception changed the personality of the game."

"We lost our poise after the Wood interception," said Kansas City lineman Jerry Mays.

The Packers continued to control the third quarter. Starr marched his offense on a 56-yard drive late in the period. He passed three times to McGee during the drive. McGee caught passes of 11 and 16 yards. Then Starr passed 13 yards to McGee for the touchdown. Chandler's fourth extra point kick gave the Packers a huge 28-10 lead.

Green Bay put together a final drive in the fourth quarter. And again it was passing by Starr that made the big plays. Starr began this drive at his own 20-yard line. He passed 25 yards to Carroll Dale. He hit McGee, again, for 37 yards. He went back to Dale for seven yards to the Kansas City 11-yard line. Runners Pitts and Taylor took over from there. Pitts scored from the one-yard line. Chandler made his fifth extra point kick. Green Bay was cleaning house, 35-10.

Bart Starr was named the first Most Valuable Player in Super Bowl history. Starr hit on 16 of 23 passes for 250 yards and two touchdowns.

He was intercepted only once. Starr's opposing quarterback, Len Dawson, also had a good game. Dawson completed 16 of 27 passes for 211 yards and one touchdown. He, too, threw one interception.

"Kansas City has a real top team," said Green Bay Coach Vince Lombardi. "But I don't think it compares with the top teams in the NFL."

"The biggest thrill is winning the game for the NFL," said running back Elijah Pitts.

"We mangled 'em a little bit," said all-star running back Jim Taylor.

The Chiefs were defeated but not silenced.

"They make mistakes," said running back Mike Garrett. "They are not superhumans. We just made more mistakes."

"They don't hit any harder than anyone else," said linebacker Sherill Headrick.

One Kansas City player might have disagreed with Headrick's comment. That was defensive back Fred "The Hammer" Williamson. All week before Super Bowl I, Williamson boasted, saying, "I am going to drop 'The Hammer' on Green Bay." In the game's fourth quarter, Williamson collided with Green Bay running back Donny Anderson. Williamson was knocked out cold. "The Hammer" had to be taken off the field on a stretcher.

On that first "Super Sunday" in Super Bowl I, Williamson's Chiefs found out just how tough the National Football League—and the Packers—played the game.

	1stQ	2ndQ	3rdQ	4thQ		Final
Kansas City	0	10	0	0	—	10
Green Bay	7	7	14	7	—	35

GB — McGee 37 pass from Starr (Chandler kick)
KC — McClinton 7 pass from Dawson (Mercer kick)
GB — Taylor 14 run (Chandler kick)
KC — FG Mercer 31
GB — Pitts 5 run (Chandler kick)
GB — McGee 13 pass from Starr (Chandler kick)
GB — Pitts 1 run (Chandler kick)

Attendance — 61,946

SUPER BOWL RECORDS

SCORING

Most Points, Game
18 Roger Craig, San Francisco, XIX

Most Touchdowns, Game
3 Roger Craig, San Francisco XIX

Most Field Goals, Game
4 Don Chandler, Green Bay, II

Longest Field Goal
48 Jan Stenerud, Kansas City, IV

BALL CARRYING

Most Yards Gained, Game
191 Marcus Allen, Los Angeles Raiders, XVIII

Longest Gain
74 Marcus Allen, Los Angeles Raiders, XVIII (TD)

PASSING

Most Yards Gained, Game
331 Joe Montana, San Francisco, XIX

Longest Completion
80 Jim Plunkett (to Kenny King), Oakland, XV (touchdown)

Most Touchdowns, Game
4 Terry Bradshaw, Pittsburgh, XIII

PASS RECEIVING

Most Receptions, Game
10 Tony Nathan, Miami, XIX

Most Yards Gained, Game
161 Lynn Swann, Pittsburgh, X

INTERCEPTIONS

Most Interceptions by, Game
3 Rod Martin, Oakland, XV

Longest Return
60 Herb Adderley, Green Bay, II (TD)

PUNTING

Longest Punt
61 Jerrel Wilson, Kansas City, I

Highest Punting Average, Game
48.5 Jerrel Wilson, Kansas City, IV (4 punts)

PUNT RETURNS

Longest Punt Return, Game
34 Darrell Green, Washington, XVIII

KICKOFF RETURNS

Longest Return, Games
98 Fulton Walker, Miami, XVII (TD)

TEAM SCORING

Most Points, Game
38 Los Angeles Raiders, XVIII; San Francisco, XIX

Fewest Points, Game
3 Miami, VI

NET YARDS GAINED

Most Yards Gained, Game
537 San Francisco, XIX

Fewest Yards Gained, Game
119 Minnesota, IX